THE INSULT DICTIONARY

How to Give 'Em Hell
in Five Nasty Languages

French
German
Spanish
Italian
English

PASSPORT BOOKS
a division of *NTC Publishing Group*
Lincolnwood, Illinois USA

To James

1995 Printing

This edition first published in 1988 by Passport Books.
© 1988, 1981 by Passport Books, a division of NTC Publishing Group,
4255 West Touhy Avenue, Lincolnwood (Chicago), Illinois 60646-1975 U.S.A.
All rights reserved. No part of this book may be reproduced, stored
in a retrieval system, or transmitted in any form or by any means,
electronic, mechanical, photocopying, recording, or otherwise,
without the prior permission of NTC Publishing Group.
Original copyright © Wolfe Publishing Ltd.
Manufactured in the United States of America.

4 5 6 7 8 9 ML 9 8 7 6 5

Preface

So you're going to a foreign country.

And you've heard that today it might not be the most pleasant experience for Americans.

You will be insulted, abused, ripped off, pushed around, frustrated—especially if you don't know the host language. That's like going to war with a slingshot. It's an invitation for every salesclerk, cabbie, waiter and bellboy (to mention a few) to take advantage of you.

That's where this marvelous little book comes in. It's your secret weapon! Its purpose is to prepare you to defend yourself against abuse. It teaches you how to take the offensive and give 'em hell, whenever necessary.

To tell people off effectively, whether in French, Italian, Spanish or German, it's not enough to rattle off a couple of words or trite expressions. You need the impact of complete expressions and sentences that put you in command. *Zingers!*

For example, if a cabbie takes you for a ride and it's time to pay the fare, wouldn't it be great to be able to say:

> "Why you big ape, you're supposed to go the
> fastest way, not the most expensive!"

And when he complains about your tip, you bounce back with:

> "The way you've been driving, you don't deserve
> what's on the meter!"

The Insult Dictionary lets you handle all infuriating situations with remarkable ease. It's simplicity itself. Just anticipate your next problem, read up on it in advance, and do battle to win! This way, when you visit a restaurant you're ready to tell the maitre d' and/or the waiter that the food is terrible, the service stinks, and the bill is outrageous! As for the language, that's easy. With each translation is a simple phonetic spelling of each expression. Just say it "like it is..." and your message will be received loud and clear. (Then you're on your own!)

Here are a few tips from the guys and gals who dared research this book:

1. Make sure the person you tell off is smaller than you, and avoid police officers.

2. Carry *The Insult Dictionary* with you at all times. It is an effective weapon, physically, as well as literally.

3. Hold onto your copy, or carry a spare. Once your traveling buddies realize the strength of this weapon, they're liable to grab yours.

Final words. Go forth. Don't defend, offend! Attack! Come back to the States victorious. Remember, you're a Yankee-Doodle Dandy. You're a high-flying flag. You're the Halls of Montezuma. So stomach in, chest out, chin up, shoulders back, and *charge!*

The Editors
PASSPORT BOOKS

NOTES ON PRONUNCIATION
by the translators

FRENCH. Most Americans are too tight-lipped to bend the mouth to produce French vowels, except after years of practice and Pernod—and even then it will betray itself. It has therefore been necessary in this dictionary to alter some French sounds to try to make them similar to English vowels. (If said pretty quickly, they almost sound like the real thing.) Here are a few notes that will help in reading the phonetic version:

Where there is 'u' in French, or 'ure', the u has been replaced by i. This must be pronounced as in 'bit' and not as in 'bite'.

The French 'j' has been translated by 'sh', but this must be pronounced fairly lightly. The word 'garage' has this sound.

The 'e', 'eu' and 'eur' sounds are expressed as 'er' or 'ehr'. Quite easy, if you lengthen them a bit. 'Euse' has been put as 'ehrz'.

Liaisons have been put in as being part of the word, in almost every case.

The 'ail' sound was the hardest to translate—'ay' dare not be used in case it was pronounced as in 'may'—so, it was decided to use 'aee' or 'a'ee'—but the ee must not be stressed.

'En', 'em', 'in', 'im', 'ein' and 'un' have all been translated by 'an' or 'am'. You can get away with it in the heat of the moment.

'Oi' by 'w', of course. Easy.

Finally, all would-be French speakers are reminded that in this delightful language *all* words are stressed on the last syllable, whatever the length.

GERMAN. The German double letter 'ß' is replaced here by 'ss'. Other usages are:

ch:	pronounce as ch in loch
g:	pronounce hard, as in 'gay'
i:	short, as in 'fit'
y:	pronounce as in 'fly'
ao:	as in 'owl'

ITALIAN. The Italian translator has produced his own system of phonetics, which should stand the one-language American in good stead. He reminds you that in Italian every vowel is pronounced.

SPANISH. *á* or *ah* is pronounced as the English *a* in *car*. (Never like *all, dare, gave*.)

é or *eh* is always like the English *e* in *set, let, wet*. (Never like *me, here, become*.)

ó or *oh* has the sound of English *o* in *lord* or English *aw* in *law*. (Never like *old, go, ago*.)

i has the sound of *i* in *bit*. (Never of *I, mine, island*.)

y has the sound of *y* in *yes, yawn*, or the *e* in *me*. (Never like *my, by, cry*.)

th has the sound of English *th* in *thing*. (Never of *the, that, this*.)

SPECIAL NOTE. As in *THE LOVER'S DICTIONARY* the translations are intended to give local equivalents or to express the same understandable idea, not to give mere literal equivalents that may mean nothing to the other person.

CONTENTS

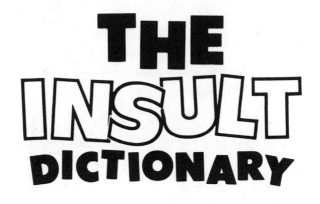

ON THE TRAIN

Two tickets to _____, please—and move it!

Bitte zwei Fahrkarten nach _____ aber schnell.

(Bitte tswy faarkaarten naach _____ aaber shhnell.)

I'd like the right change, if you don't mind.

Ich hätte gerne das richtige Wechselgeld, wenn's Ihnen nichts ausmacht.

(Ish haette gairne daas reechtige vaychslgeld, vens eenen neechts aosmaacht.)

Is this a passenger car or a garbage truck?

Soll das ein Eisenbahnwagen oder ein Müllwagen sein?

(Zoll daas eyn eysenbaanvaagen oder eyn muellvaagen seyn.)

I asked for a porter, not a pygmy.

Ich brauche einen Gepäckträger, keinen Zwerg.

(Ish braoch eynen Gepaektraeger keynen tsverg.)

Do your trains ever run on time?

Fahren Ihre Züge je pünktlich?

(Faaren eere Tsuege yea puenktlich.)

What do you mean, the tip isn't enough? It's twice as much as you deserve.

Was, das Trinkgeld genügt Ihnen nicht? Sie verdienen höchstens die Hälfte.

(Vass, daass Trinkgayld genuegt eenen neecht? Zee ferdeenen hoechstens dee Haelfte.)

FRENCH	ITALIAN	SPANISH

FRENCH

Deux billets pour _____ s'il vous plaît, et que ça saute!

(Der beeyeh poor _____ seel voo play, eh ksa sawt!)

ITALIAN

Due biglietti per _____ per favore, e possiamo spicciarci?

(Doo-eh beelliet-tee per _____ per favore, eh posseeamo speech-charchee?)

SPANISH

Deme dos billetes, por favor, y váyase al cuerno.

(Démeh dós beelytes, pór fahbór ee báyaseh ál kwérnoh.)

Je ne refuserai pas la monnaie exacte, vous savez!

(Shern refizray par la mawnay exact, voo savay!)

Il resto lo gradirei giusto, se non le dispiace.

(Eel resto lo gradeeray jewsto, se non leh dee-(speea-cheh.)

Le agradecería que me devolviese bien el cambio, si no le importa.

(Leh agradetheriya ke meh debolbiéseh bién él kámbeeyo, see no lé eempórtah.)

C'est un wagon de voyageurs ou un fourgon à bestiaux?

(Stan vagon der vwayasher oo an foorgon ah bestio?)

Questo è un vagone ferroviario, o un carro bestiame?

(Kwesto eh un vagone ferroveeah-reeo, oh oon carro best-eea-meh?)

¿Esto es un vagón de tren, o el carro de la basura?

(Éstoh éss oon bagón dé trén oh él kárroh dé lah bahsoorah?)

Je veux un porteur, pas un gringalet!

(Sher ver an portehr, pazan grangallay!)

Ho bisogno di un facchino non di un pigmeo.

(Oh beesonio dee oon fakkeeno non dee oon pigmehoh.)

He pedido un mozo, no un mequetrefe.

(Eh pedidoh oon móthaw, noh oon meketréfeh.)

Est-ce qu'il leur arrive d'être à l'heure, vos trains?

(Ayskeel lehr arreev daytr ah lehr, vo tran?)

Ma i vostri treni viaggiano *mai* in orario?

(Mah ee vostree tre-nee veea-jah-noh maee in orareeo?)

¿A qué hora sale el tren, cuando le da la gana?

(Ah ké óra sáleh él trén, kwandoh leh dá lah gánah?)

Qu'est-ce que tu veux dire, le pourboire n'est pas assez? Pour ce que t'as fait, c'est deux fois trop!

(Kaysker ti ver deer, lehr poorbwar nay par zassay? Poor sker tar fay, say der fwar tro!)

La mancia non le basta? Per quel che ha fatto è già il doppio di quel che si merita.

(La man-cha non leh bahstah? Per kwel keh ah fatto eh ja eel dop-peeo dee kwel keh see meritah.)

¿No tiene bastante propina? ¡Por lo que ha hecho, es el doble de la que merece!

(Noh tyéneh bastánteh propeenah? Pór loh ké ah étchoh, éss él dóble dé lah ké meréthe!)

ON THE TRAIN

This car stinks!

Dieses Abteil stinkt.
(Deeses Ubtyl shtinkt.)

What do you mean, the suitcases are too heavy?

Wieso ist das Gepäck zu schwer, haben Sie denn keine Kraft?
(Veeso eest daas Gepaek tsu shvair, haaben Zee denn keyne Kraaft.)

This car is filthy!

Dieser Wagen ist dreckig.
(Deeser Vaagen eest drekeeg.)

What do you mean, the suitcases are too heavy?

FRENCH	ITALIAN	SPANISH

FRENCH

Ça pue, ce wagon!
(Sar pi, sehr vagon!)

Qu'est-ce que tu veux dire, ces valises sont trop lourdes? T'as pas de muscles?
(Kaysker ti ver deer, say valeez son traw loord? Tar par d'miskl?)

C'est une vraie porcherie, ce wagon!
(Stin vray porsheree, sehr vagon!)

ITALIAN

Questo vagone puzza.
(Kwesto vah-goh-neh poot-zah.)

Sono troppo pesanti queste valigie? Ma lei al posto dei muscoli cos'ha?
(Sono troppo peh-zan-tee kwe-steh vahlee-je? Ma lay al posto day mooscolee cos-ah?)

Questo vagone è lurido.
(Kwesto vah-goh-neh eh looreedo.)

SPANISH

Este vagón apesta.
(Ésteh bagón apéstah.)

No me diga que pesa demasiado. Lo que pasa es que es usted un enclenque.
(Noh meh deegah ke péssah demmassiádoh. Loh ké pássah éss ké oostéh éss oon enklénkeh.)

Este vagón es una porquería.
(Ésteh bagón éss oona porkereea.)

ON THE TRAIN

Do you want us to freeze to death?
Shut that window!

Sollen wir alle erfrieren. Machen Sie mal das Fenster zu.

(Zollen veer aalle airfreeren. Maachen Zee maal daass Fenster tsu.)

Give me that rag. This seat isn't a footstool.

Geben Sie mir das Tuch. Müssen Sie Ihre Füsse auf den Sitz legen.

(Gaybn Zee meer daas` Tooch. Muessen Zee eere Fuesse aof den Zeets laygen.)

You may be fat enough for two seats, but you only paid for one. Move over!

Sie sind zwar dick genug für zwei, aber Sie haben nur für einen Platz gezahlt Rücken Sie weiter.

(Zee sind tsvaar dick genoog fuer tswy, aaber Zee haaben noor fuer eynen Platts getsaalt Rueken Zee vyter.)

Get your big feet out of my way!

Nehmen Sie mal Ihre Latschen weg.

(Naymen Zee maal eere Laatshen vayg.)

How much room do you really need?

Wieviel Platz brauchen Sie eigentlich?

(Veefeel Plaats baochen Zee eygentlich?)

Put that great big suitcase over your own fat head. I don't want it falling on me.

Diesen grossen Koffer legen Sie mal über Ihren Platz. Ich sehe nicht ein, dass er auf mich fallen soll.

(Deesen grossen Koffer laygen Zee maal ueber eeren Plaats. Ish sayhe neecht eyn, daass er aof meech faallen zol.)

FRENCH	ITALIAN	SPANISH
Tu veux nous faire crever de froid? Ferme cette fenêtre!	Dobbiamo morire tutti congelati? Chiuda quel finestrino.	¿Quiere matarnos de frío? ¡Cierre la ventana!
(Ti ver noo fair krervay d'frwar? Fehrm set fernaytr!)	*(Dob-beea-mo mo-ree-reh toot-tee con-jeh-la-tee? Kew-dah kwel fee-ne-streeno.)*	*(Kyéreh matárnos dé freeyo? Theeyerreh lah bentánah!)*
Passe-moi ce torchoń. C'est une banquette, pas un repose-pied!	Mi dia quello straccio. Quello è un sedile non un poggia-piedi.	Quite las pezuñas. Este asiento no es un taburete.
(Pass-mwar sehr torshon. Stin bankett, par zan rerpoze-peeay!)	*(Mee deeah kwello strachcho. Kwello eh oon seh-dee-leh non oon poj-jah pee-eh-dee.)*	*(Keetteh lás pethoonyas. Esteh assyéntoh noh éss oon tabooréteh.)*
T'es assez gros pour occuper deux places, mais t'en a payé qu'une—bouge-toi!	È vero che lei è grasso abbastanza per due posti, ma ne ha pagato uno solo. Si muova.	Está tan gordo que necesita dos asientos, pero sólo ha pagado una plaza. Quítese de ahí.
(Tay assay groh poor occupay der plass, may tana payay kin—boosh-twa!)	*(Eh vehro keh lay eh grahsso aab-bah-stahn-tzah per dooeh pohstee, mah neh ah pahgah-toh oonoh solo. See moo-oh-vah.)*	*(Stá tán górdoh ke nethesseetah dós assyéntos, péroh sóloh ah pagádoh oona plathah. Keeteseh dé akee.)*
Tire donc tes panards d'là!	Levi di mezzo le sue piote.	Quite las patas de en medio.
(Teer donk tay panar d'lar!)	*(Leh-vee dee metzo leh soo-eh pee-oh-teh.)*	*(Keeteh lás pátas deh én médeeoh.)*
Combien de place tu crois qu'il te faut?	Allora ha deciso quanto posto le occorre?	¿Cuánto sitio cree usted que necesita?
(Kombyen d'plass ti crwa keel ter faw?)	*(Allorah ah deh-chee-soh kwanto posto leh oc-correh?)*	*(Kwántoh seettyoh kré-eh oostéh ké netheseetah?)*
Fous donc cette grosse valise au-dessus de ta tête! Je ne vois pas pourquoi je la recevrais sur la mienne!	Metta quella enorme valigia sopra la sua zucca—non vedo proprio perché debba cadere su di me.	Ponga su asquerosa maleta encima de su cabeza. No quiero que se me caiga encima.
(Foo donk set gros valeez od'si der tar tayt! Shern vwar par poorkwar shlar rerssvray sir lar myen!)	*(Meht-tah kwella ehnormeh vah-lee-jah sohpra la soo-ah tzooc-cah—non veh-doh proh-preeo pehr-keh dehb-bah cah-dehreh soo dee meh.)*	*(Póngah soo asskerósah mahlétah entheemah dé soo kabétha. Noh kyéroh ké sé mé káigah entheemah.)*

ON THE TRAIN

Open that window before we all choke to death.

Machen Sie das Fenster auf, bevor wir alle ersticken.

(Maachen Zee daas Fenster aof, befor veer aalle airshteeken.)

Put that smelly cigarette out—this is a no-smoking car.

Drücken Sie Ihre lausige Zigarette aus, das ist ein Nichtraucher.

(Drueken Zee eere laozeege Tseegarette aos, daas eest eyn Neechtraocher.)

If you don't like the smell of my pipe, you know what you can do.

Sie können mich mal, wenn Ihnen mein Pfeifengeruch nicht passt.

(Zee koennen meech maal, venn eenen myn Pfyfengerooch neecht passt.)

ON BOARD SHIP

I asked for a cabin, not a closet.

Ich habe eine Kabine verlangt, keinen Schrank.

(Ish haabe eyne Kaabeene ferlaangt, kynen Shraank.)

Please spill your soup on somebody else.

Schütten Sie die Suppe nicht ausgerechnet über mich.

(Shuetten Zee dee Soupe neecht ousgereychnet ueber meesh.)

This cabin is disgusting.

Das ist eine elende Kabine.

(Daas eest eyne aylende Kaabeene.)

FRENCH	ITALIAN	SPANISH
Ouvre donc cette fenêtre avant qu'on crève pour de bon! *(Oovr'er donk set fernaytr avan kon craiv poor der bon!)*	Apra il finestrino prima che moriamo tutti soffocati. *(Ahprah eel fee-neh-stree-noh preema keh moreeahmo toot-tee sof-foh-cah-tee.)*	Abra la ventana antes de que nos ahoguemos de calor. *(Abrah lah bentánah ántess dé ké nós aoguémos de kalór.)*
Eh eh, là, la cigarette— c'est un non-fumeur ici! *(Eh eh, lar, lar seeğaret— stan non-fimehr eessee!)*	Spenga quella sigaretta puzzolente, qui è vietato fumare. *(Spehngah kwella see-gah-reht-tah pootz-oh-lenteh, kwee eh vee-eh-ta-to foomareh.)*	Tire esta colilla de una vez. Aquí es para no fumadores. *(Teereh éstah koleelya deh oona béth. Akee éss párah nó foomahdóres.)*
Si t'aimes pas l'odeur de ma pipe, t'as qu'à te tirer! *(See taym par lodehr d'mar peep, tar kar t'teeray!)*	Se non le aggrada il pro-fumo della mia pipa, peggio per lei. *(Seh non leh aggradah eel proh-foomoh dehlla mee-ah pee-pah, peh-joh per lay.)*	Si no le gusta el humo de mi pipa, lárguese de aquí. *(See nó leh goostah él oomoh deh mee peepah, lárgueseh dé akee.)*
J'ai demandé une cabine, pas un placard! *(Shay d'manday in cabeen, pazan plakahr!)*	Voglio una cabina, non un armadio. *(Voh-llioh oonah cah-bee-nah, non oon ar-mah-deeoh.)*	He pedido un camarote, no una alacena. *(Eh pedidoh oon kamah-róteh, nó oona alahthénah.)*
Allez flanquer votre soupe sur quelqu'un d'autre, s'il vous plaît! *(Allay flankay votsoop sir kelkan dawtr, seel voo play!)*	Le dispiace versare la minestra su qualcun altro? *(Leh dee-speeah-che vesareh la mee-neh-strah soo kwal-coon altroh?)*	Manche de sopa a su tía, ¿quiere? *(Mántche dé sópah ah soo teeah, kyéreh?)*
Cette cabine est dégoû-tante! *(Set cabeen ay daigootant!)*	Questa cabina fa schifo. *(Kwestah cah-bee-nah fa skee-foh.)*	Este camarote es un asco. *(Ésteh kamahróteh ess oon ásskoh.)*

ON BOARD SHIP

Captain, were you in charge of a rowboat before?

Waren Sie bisher Kapitän eines Ruderboots oder eines Vergnügungsdampfers?

(Vaarn Zee bishair Kaapitaen eynes Rooderboats oder eynes Fergnuegoongsdaampfers.)

Please get your filthy toilet articles out of my way; I'm free of disease and I intend to stay that way.

Nehmen Sie gefälligst Ihr drekkiges Waschzeug weg, ich will mich nicht infizieren.

(Naymen Zee gefaelligst eer dreckeeges Vashtsoig vag, ish vil meesh neecht infeetseeren.)

Steward, are you sure it wasn't too much trouble waking up? It's only lunchtime, you know.

Steward, hoffentlich habe ich nicht, Ihren Schlaf gestört, aber es ist bereits Mittag.

(Steward, hoffentleesh haabe ish neecht eeren Shlaaf gestooert, aaber as eest beryts Mittaag.)

Why would I want to sit at the Captain's table? To listen to his idiotic ramblings?

Ich hab keine Lust, am Tisch des Kapitäns zu sitzen und mir sein uninteressantes Gequassel anzuhören.

(Ish haab keyne Loost am Tish des Kapitaens tsu seetsen oond mir syn ooninteressaantes Gequaasl antsuhoeren.)

Take my suitcase and hurry up!

Nehmen Sie meinen Koffer und beeilen Sie sich.

(Naymen Zee mynen Kofer oond beeylen Zee seech.)

FRENCH	ITALIAN	SPANISH
Capitaine, vous commandiez un bateau à rames ou bien c'était un bateau-mouche?	Scusi capitano, lei prima comandava una barca a remi, o un vaporetto da diporto?	Capitán, ¿mandaba usted un bote de remos o un barquito de vela?
(Capeetayn, voo commandeeay in bartoh ar' rahm oo byen saitay tan bartohmoosh?)	*(Scoosee cah-pee-tah-noh, lay preema coh-man-dah-vah oona barcah ah reh-mee oh oon vah-poh-reht-toh dah deeportoh?)*	*(Capeetán, mandábah oostéh oon bóteh dé rémos oh oon barkeetoh dé bélah?)*
Enlevez vos sales articles de toilette d'ici, je n'ai aucune maladie pour l'instant.	Tolga di mezzo i suoi sporchi articoli di toilette. Per ora sto benissimo e non intendo certo prendere delle malattie.	Quite de ahí sus trastos de aseo, no quiero ponerme malo todavía.
Anl'vay vaw sarl zarteekl'er der twalet deecee, shnay awkin mahlahdee poor lanstan.)	*(Tolgah dee meh-tzoh ee soo-oh-ee spohr-kee arteecolee dee too-ah-let. Per oh-rah stoh beh-nees-seemoh eh non intendoh chertoh prehn-deh-reh dehlleh mahlah-tee-eh.*	*(Keeteh dé akee soos trastos dé asséoh, nó kyéroh ponérmeh máloh toddabeea.)*
Steward, vous êtes sûr qu'il n'est pas trop tôt pour vous réveiller, il n'est que midi, vous savez?	Cameriere, è sicuro di non essersi svegliato troppo presto? Dopotutto è solo mezzogiorno.	Camarero, ¿no le molestaría despertarme, si es que se levanta antes de mediodía?
(Steewahr, voo zet sir keel nay par tro toe poor voo raivayay, eel nay k'meedee, voo savay?)	*(Cah-meh-ree-eh-reh, eh see-co-roh dee non essersee sveh-lliatoh troppoh prehstoh? Doh-poh toot-toh eh solo metzo-jornoh.)*	*(Kamahréroh, nó leh molestareeya despertármeh, see ess ke seh lebántah ántess de meddiohdea?)*
Pourquoi voulez-vous que je me mette à la table du Capitaine? Pour écouter ses radotages?	E perché dovrei voler mangiare alla tavola del capitano? Per sentire quei suoi discorsi idioti?	¿Para qué he de sentarme a la mesa del capitán? ¿Para oir sus malditas correrías?
(Poorkwar voolay-voo ker shmer met ar la tahbl'er di Capeetayn? Poor aycootay say rahdotarsh?)	*(Eh per-keh dovray voler man-ja-reh alla tah-voh-lah dehl cah-pee-tah-noh? Per senteereh kwe-ee soo-oh-ee deescorsee idiot-ee?*	*(Párah ké eh dé sentármeh ah lah mésah dél kapeetán? Párah oeer soos maldeetas kohrrereeas?)*
Allez, ramasse ma valise et fais vite!	Prenda quella mia valigia e non perda tempo.	Tome estas maletas y despáchese pronto.
(Allay, ramass mar valeez ay fay veet!)	*Prendah kwella mee-ah vahlee-jah e non per-dah tempo.)*	*(Tómeh éstas mahlétas ce despátcheseh próntoh.)*

ON BOARD SHIP

Just because you're an officer, you think you're a big shot.

Sie glauben wohl Sie sind als Schiffsoffizier was besonderes.

(Zee glaoben vol Zee sind aals Shiffsoffeetseer vaas baysonderes.)

Get out of my cabin, you hairy ape.

Machen Sie, dass Sie aus meiner Kabine kommen, Sie mieser Kunde.

(Maachen Zee, daass Zee aos myner Kaabeene komen, Zee meezer Koonde.)

Now I understand why everyone flies these days.

Es ist mir jetzt völlig klar, warum heute jeder fliegt.

(As eest meer yatst foellig klaar vaaroom hoite yeader fleegt.)

I know the boat is rocking, but when I ask for a double, I mean a double.

Schön, das Schiff schaukelt, deshalb brauchen Sie mir aber doch nicht einen kleinen Gin zu geben, wenn ich einen grossen bestelle.

(Shoen, daas Shiff shaokelt, deshaalb braochen Zee meer aaber dosh neecht eynen klynen gin tsu geyben, venn ish eynen grossen beyshtelle.)

This isn't just second-class; it's a disgrace.

Das ist nicht nur zweite Klasse sondern auch jämmerlich.

(Daas eest neecht noor tswyte Klaasse zondern aoch yaemmerlish.)

FRENCH	ITALIAN	SPANISH

Simplement parce que vous êtes un officier, vous vous prenez pour une grosse merde?

(Samplehrman pahrsker voo zet zan offeesyay, voo voo prehrnay poor in gross maird?)

Cosa crede lei, di essere onnipotente solo perché è un ufficiale?

(Coh-sah creh-deh lay, dee essereh ohn-nee-poh-tehn-teh solo perkeh eh oon oof-fee-cha-leh?)

¡A ver si porque es un oficial se cree Don Juan de Austria!

(Ah bér see porké ess oon offithiál sé cré-eh Don Whwán dé Owstria!)

Fous le camp de ma cabine, espèce de macaque!

(Fool kam d'mar cabeen, espays de makark!)

Esca subito dalla mia cabina, scimmione peloso.

(Escah soo-bee-toh dahllah mee-ah cah-bee-nah, shee-meeo-neh peh-loh-soh.)

Salga de mi camarote, pedazo de alcornoque.

(Sálgah dé mee kamah-róteh, pedátho dé alkor-nókeh.)

Je comprends maintenant pourquoi tout le monde prend l'avion.

(Shkompran mantnan poorkwar tool mond pran lavyon!)

Adesso capisco perché oggigiorno tutti vanno in aeroplano.

(Ah-dehsso cah-pee-scoh perkeh ojjee-jornoh toot-tee vahnno in ah-eh-roh-planoh.)

Ahora comprendo porque todo el mundo va en avión.

(Ah-óra kompréndoh porké tódoh el moondo bah én abeeón.)

Je sais bien que le bateau roule, mais quand je demande un double gin, c'est bien un double gin que je veux, pas un dé à coudre!

(Shsay byen kerl bartoh rool, may kan sh'dermand in doobl'er gin, say byen an doobl'er gin kersh vehr, pazan day ar coodr!)

Lo so che c'è un rullio tremendo, ma quando chiedo un doppio gin non mi aspetto la misura di un ditale.

(Loh soh keh che oon roolleeo treh-men-doh, mah kwando kee-eh-doh oon dop-peeoh gin non mee ah-speht-toh la mee-soo-rah dee oon dee-taleh.)

Ya sé que el barco se balancea, pero cuando pido una ginebra doble no quiero un dedalito.

(Yah sé ké él bárcoh seh balánthéa, péroh kwandoh peedoh oona heenébrah dóbleh no kyéroh oon dehdaleetoh.)

C'est pas seulement une deuxième classe, c'est de la pourriture!

(Say par sehrlman in derzyaim klarss, say d'lar pooreetir!)

Questa non è una seconda classe, è una degradazione.

(Kwestah non eh oonah seh-con-dah clahs-seh, eh oonah deh-grah-dah-tzee-oh-neh.)

Esto no es Segunda Clase, es una degradación.

(Estoh nó éss segoondah clásse, éss oona degrada-thión.)

IN THE TAXI

It's my taxi—I waved first.

Das ist mein Taxi, ich hab's zuerst gerufen.
(*Daas eest myn taksi, ish haabs tsuairst geroofn.*)

Not so fast, you idiot.

Nicht so schnell, Sie Idiot.
(*Neecht zo shnell, Zee Eediot.*)

Can't you go faster, you fool?

Fahren Sie doch nicht im Schnekkentempo, Sie Narr.
(*Faaren Zee dosh neecht im Shnaykentempo, Zee Naarr.*)

You're supposed to take the quickest way—not the most expensive.

Fahren Sie gefälligst den kürzesten, nicht den teuersten Weg.
(*Faaren Zee gefelligst den kuertsesten, neecht den toyersten Vayg.*)

What do you mean, the tip isn't big enough—the way you've been driving you don't deserve what's on the meter.

Das Trinkgeld genügt Ihnen nicht—für Ihr Fahren verdienen Sie nicht einmal den Betrag auf der Zähluhr.
(*Daas Trinkgayld genuegt eenen neecht—fuer eer faaren ferdeenen Zee neecht eynmaal den Betraag aof der Tsayloor.*)

How many people have you killed today?

Wieviele Menschen haben Sie denn heute schon überfahren?
(*Vi feele Manshen haaben Zee denn hoite shon ueberfaaren?*)

FRENCH	ITALIAN	SPANISH
Il est à moi ce taxi, j'ai fait signe avant vous. *(Eel ay tar mwar staxee, shay fay seen avan voo!)*	Questo tassí è mio, l'ho chiamato prima io. *(Kwesto taxi eh mee-o, l'oh kia-mah-to pree-mah ee-o.)*	Es mi taxi, lo llamé primero. *(Ess mee táxi, loh lyahmé preeméroh.)*
Eh, vas-y mollo, vieüx! *(Eh, vazee molo, vyer.)*	Non corra tanto, idiota. *(Non cor-rah tahn-to, idiot-ah.)*	¡No corra tánto, idiota! *(Noh kórrah tántoh, eedió-tah!)*
Eh dis, c'est un escargot que tu suis? *(Eh dee, stan eskargoe k'ti swee?)*	Non può andare piú in fretta di una lumaca, pelandrone? *(Non poo-oh ahn-dah-reh pew in freh-ttah dee oona loo-mah-ca, peh-lahn-droneh?)*	¿Piensa ir todo el tiempo a paso de tortuga, imbécil? *(Peeyénsah eer tóddoh él teeyémpoh ah pásoh dé tor-toogah, imbéthill?)*
Vous êtes censé prendre le chemin le plus court, et non pas le plus cher. *(Voo zet sansay prandr'er lehr shman lehr pli coor, ay non par lehr pli shair!)*	Le dispiace prendere la via piú diretta, non quella piú cara? *(Leh dee-spee-ah-cheh prehn-deh-reh lah vee-ah pew dee-reh-ttah, non kweh-llah, pew cah-rah?)*	Le he dicho que tome el camino más corto, no el más caro. *(Leh eh deetchoh ké tómeh él cammeenoh máss kórtoh, noh él máss károh.)*
Qu'est-ce que ça veut dire, c'est pas assez comme pourboire? De la façon dont vous avez conduit, vous ne méritez même pas ce qu'il y a sur le compteur! *(Kaysker sar vehr deer, say par zassay kom poorbwar? D'lar farson don voo zavay kondwee, voon maireetay maim par skeel yah sir lehr kontehr!)*	Come, la mancia non le basta? Ha guidato in un modo tale che non si merita neanche quel che segna il tassametro. *(Co-meh, lah mahn-chah non leh bah-sta? Ah goo-ee-dah-to in oon modo tah-leh keh non see merit-ah neh-ahn-keh kwehl keh seh-niah eel tah-ssah-metro.)*	¡Ya está bién de propina! De la forma que conduce no merece ni lo que marca el taxímetro. *(Yah stá beeyén deh prop-peenah! Dé lá fórmah ké kondoêthe noh mehréthe nee loh ké márcah él taxímetroh.)*
Vous en avez tué combien aujourd'hui? *(Voo zan avay tiay kom-byen oshoordwee?)*	Quante altre persone ha ucciso oggi? *(Kwahn-teh al-treh person-eh ah oo-chees-o oh-djee?)*	¿A cuántos ha matado hoy? *(Ah kwántoss ah mahtá-doh óy?)*

23

IN THE TAXI

I've seen some speeding in my time, but nothing like your meter.

Geschwindigkeit kenne ich, aber Ihre rasende Zähluhr schlägt alles. Wie haben Sie die hingebogen?

(Gayshvindigkeyt kanne ish, aaber eere raazende Tsayloor shlaegt aalles, vi haaben Zee dee hingaybohgen?)

Ten percent is more than enough; you don't deserve anything.

Zehn Prozent ist mehr als genug, an sich gebührt Ihnen gar nichts.

(Tsayn Protsent eest mair aals genoog, an seesh gebuert eenen gaar neechts.)

Are you color-blind? That was a red light.

Sind Sie farbenblind, die Verkehrsampel war rot.

(Zind Zee faarbenbleend, dee Ferkairsaampl vaar roht.)

Do you make your passengers take out accident insurance?

Ihre Fahrgäste benötigen wohl eine Sonder-Unfallversicherung?

(Eere Faargaeste benoeteegen vol eyne Zonder-Oonfaallferseesherung.)

No, I don't want to share my cab with a fat slob like you; there's hardly enough room for one person.

Es fällt mir gar nicht ein, das Taxi mit einem so dicken Kerl wie Sie zu teilen, hier ist ja kaum Platz für eine Person.

(Es faellt meer gaar neecht eyn, daas Taksi mit eynem zo dicken Kairl vi Zee tsu tylen, heer eest yaa kaom Plaatz fuer eyne pairsohn.)

FRENCH	ITALIAN	SPANISH

FRENCH

J'en ai vu des trucs rapides dans ma vie, mais jamais comme votre compteur. Comment faites-vous?

(Shan ay vi day trik rahpeed dan mar vee, may jarmay kom vawtr kontehr. Koman fait-voo?)

ITALIAN

Ne ho viste correre di macchine, ma non ho mai visto un tassametro andare cosí in fretta. È un suo brevetto?

(Neh oh vee-steh coh-rreh-reh dee mah-kkee-neh, mah non oh my vee-sto oon tah-ssah-metro ah-ndah-reh cozi in freh-tah. Eh oon soo-o breh-veh-to?)

SPANISH

He visto correr muchas cosas, pero ninguna como su taxímetro. ¡A ver si lo arregla!

(Eh beestoh korrér mootchas kóssas, péroh neengoonah kómoh soo taxímetroh. Ah bér see loh arréglah!)

Dix-pour-cent, c'est plus que suffisant, en fait vous ne méritez rien du tout.

Dee-poor-san, say plik sifizan, an fait voon maireetay ryèn di too!)

Dieci per cento è piú che sufficiente. Del resto non si merita nulla.

(Dee-eh-chee pehr chen-to eh pew keh soo-fee-chehn-teh. Del rest-o non see merit-a noo-llah.)

Un diez por ciento y basta . . . No se merece ni esto.

(Oon deeyéth pór theeyénto y básstah . . . Noh sé mehréthe nee éstoh.)

Eh! Vous ne distinguez pas les couleurs? C'était un feu rouge!

(Eh! Voon deestangay par lay coolehr? Stay tan fehr roosh!)

Ma lei è daltonico? Quel semaforo era rosso.

(Mah lay eh dahl-tó-nee-co? Kwehl seh-mah-phoro eh-ra ro-sso.)

¿Está ciego? Ha pasado con luz roja.

(Stá thiëgoh? Ah passádoh kón looth róhha.)

Est-ce que vous faites prendre à vos clients des polices d'assurance spéciales?

(Aysker voo fait prandr'ar vo cleean day polees dassirans spayseearl?)

Prima di viaggiare con lei i suoi clienti si assicurano la vita?

(Preema dee vee-ah-djahreh con lay ee soo-oh-ee clee-ehn-tee see ah-ssee-coorahno lah vee-ta?)

¡Oiga! ¿Hay que firmar una póliza de seguro para subir a este taxi?

(Óygah! Ay keh feermár oona pólithah deh seggooroh párah soobeer ah éste táxi?)

Non, je ne veux pas partager mon taxi avec des patapoufs de votre espèce, y a déjà pas assez de place pour une personne.

(Non, shern vehr par partashay mon taxee aveck day pattapoof der vawtr espays, yar dayshar par zassay d'plars poor in person.)

No, non intendo condividere questo tassí con un grassone come lei. Non c'è quasi posto per me.

(No, non intend-oh con-dee-vee-deh-reh kwesto taxi con oon grass-oh-neh coh-meh lay. Non cheh kwah-see posto per meh.)

No. No quiero a un tipo tan gordo en el taxi. Sólo hay sitio para uno.

(Noh. Noh kyéroh ah oon teepoh tán górdon én él táxi. Sóloh áy seetyoh párah oonoh.)

ON THE BUS

Just wait your turn, you ill-mannered slob.

Drängen Sie sich nicht vor, Sie ungeschliffener Banause.
(Drayngen zee zich nicht for, zee oongeshliffener baanaose.)

Hurray, you finally showed up.

Hurra! Da bist Du ja endlich.
(Hoorraa! daa bist doo yaa endlich.)

What kept you?

Was hat Dich aufgehalten?
(Vaass hat deech aofgehaalten?)

There's plenty of room inside.

Da drin ist massenhaft Platz.
(Daa drinn ist maassenhaft plats.)

Your rear end is big enough for three seats, but you only bought one ticket. Move over!

Ihr Hinterteil ist gross genug für drei Sitze, Sie haben aber nur 'ne Kinderkarte—also rücken Sie 'mal.
(Eer hintertyl ist gros genoog fuer dry zitse, zee haaben aaber noor 'na keendrkaarte—aalzo ruekken zee 'maal.)

Please cough all over your own family— I don't need your germs.

Seien Sie so nett und beehren Sie Ihre eigene Familie mit Ihren Bakterien. Ich will sie nicht.
(Zyen zee zo nett oond be-eren zee eere ygene faameelee-a meet eeren baktayrian. Ich vil zee nicht.)

Get your dirty hand off my behind.

Nehmen Sie Ihre widerliche Hand von meinem Hintern weg.
(Naymen zee eere veederliche haand fon mynem hintern vayg.)

FRENCH	ITALIAN	SPANISH
Eh! Attends donc ton tour, paysan! *(Eh! Attan donk ton toor, paysan!)*	Aspetti il suo turno, zoticone maleducato. *(Ahs-peh-tee eel soo-oh toor-no, tzo-tee-ko-neh mah-leh-doo-cah-to.)*	¡Póngase en la cola, mal educado! *(Póngaseh én lah kawla, mál eddokádoh!)*
Bravo! Te voilà enfin! *(Bravo! Ter vwalah an-fan!)*	Evviva! Finalmente ci siete. *(Eh-vee-vah! Fee-nahl-mehn-teh chee see-eh-teh!)*	¡Vaya! ¡Nunca es tarde cuándo llega! *(Báyah! Noonkah éss tár-deh kwándoh lyégah!)*
Qu'est-ce qui t'as retardé? *(Kayskee tar retarday?)*	Cosa vi ha trattenuto? *(Cosah vee ah trah-tteh-noo-to?)*	¿A qué espera? *(Ah keh spérah?)*
Il y a de la place en pagaye! *(Eel ya d'lar plars an paga'ee.)*	Ma c'è ancora tanto posto! *(Mah cheh ahn-córah tah-nto po-sto!)*	¡Pase adentro! ¿No ve que hay sitio? *(Pásseh adéntroh! Noh béh keh áy seettyoh?)*
Je sais bien qu'il te faut trois places pour mettre ton cul, mais t'as payé qu'une demi-place. Serre-toi un peu. *(Sh'say byen keel ter faw trwar plars poor metr'er ton ky, may tar payay kin demi-plars. Sair-twar an pehr.)*	Ci vorrebbero tre posti per il suo sedere, però ne ha solo pagato mezzo. Si sposti. *(Chee vo-rrheh-bbeh-ro treh post-ee per eel soo-oh seh-deh-reh, peh-róh neh ah pa-gah-to solo meh-tzo. See spost-ee.)*	Su trasero vale por tres, pero sólo ha pagado un billete. ¡Déjeme sitio! *(Soo trasséroh báhle pór trés, péroh sóloh ah pagádoh oon beelyéteh. Déhhemeh seettyoh!)*
Allez tousser et répandre vos microbes en famille s'il vous plaît, j'en veux pas! *(Allay toossay ay raypan-dr'er vaw meekrob an fa-meey'er, seel voo play, shan vehr par!)*	Quando tossisce per favore tenga i suoi germi in famiglia, io non li desidero. *(Kwah-ndo to-see-sheh per fah-voreh teh-ngah ee soo-o-ee germ-ee in family-a, eeo non lee deh-zee-dero.)*	Vaya a toser a su casa. Aquí no queremos microbios. *(Báyah ah tossér ah soo kássa. Akkee noh kehrémos meecróbyos.)*
Mets donc pas tes sales pattes sur mon derrière! *(May donk par tay sal pat sir mon dereeayr!)*	Tenga le mani in tasca, porcaccione. *(Tehn-gah leh ma-nee in tah-scah, pork-ah-cho-neh.)*	Quíteme las manos de encima. *(Keetemeh láss mános deh entheemah.)*

ON THE BUS

Congratulations, driver, we finally reached five miles an hour.

Gratuliere—Sie haben's wahrhaftig geschafft, im Fünf-Kilometer-Tempo zu fahren.

(Graatooleere—zee haaben's vaarhaftig geshaafft, im fuenf-keelomayter-tempo tsoo faaren.)

You've gone past my stop, you jerk.

Sie Trottel, Sie sind an der Haltestelle vorbeigefahren.

(Zee trottle, zee sind an dair haalteshtelle forby-gefaaren.)

***To the driver:* When did you last have your eyes checked? Was it twenty years ago? Or maybe fifty?**

TO THE DRIVER: Wann waren Sie zuletzt beim Augenarzt? Vor zwanzig Jahren oder vor fünfzig?

(TO THE DRIVER: vaann vaaren zee tsoolaytst bym aogenaartst? for tsvanssig yaaren oder for fuenfssig?)

***To the conductor:* How about the rest of my change, you crook?**

TO THE CONDUCTOR: Und wo ist das andere Wechselgeld, Sie Gauner?

(TO THE CONDUCTOR: Oond vo ist daass aandere vaykselgayld, zee gaoner?)

ON THE SUBWAY

Please breathe your garlic in somebody else's face.

Pusten Sie, bitte, jemanden anderen mit Ihrem Knoblauch an.

(Poosten zee, bitte, yaymaanden aandren meet eerem cnoblaoch aan.)

FRENCH	ITALIAN	SPANISH
Félicitations, chauffeur! Vous êtes arrivé à faire exactement du cinq à l'heure! *(Fayleeceetasyon, shaufehr! Voo zet zareevay ar fair exacterman di sank ar lehr!)*	I miei complimenti conducente, in quel punto ha superato i cinque chilometri orari. *(Ee mee-eh-ee compliment-ee, con-doo-chen-teh, in kweh-l poon-to ah soo-per-ah-to ee cheen-kweh kilo-meh-tree orah-ree.)*	Le felicito, chófer. Por lo menos vamos a diez por hora. *(Leh fehlithitoh, chóffeur. Pór loh ménos bámos ah dyéth pór órah.)*
Eh, chauffard! Et mon arrêt? *(Eh, shaufahr! Ay mon array?)*	Sciagurato, non vede che ha passato la fermata? *(Shah-goo-rah-to, non veh-deh keh ah pah-ssah-to lah feh-rmah-ta?)*	¿Por qué no se detiene en la parada, memo? *(Pór keh noh seh detyéneh én lah parádah, mémoh?)*
TO THE DRIVER: Quand est-ce que vous êtes passé pour la dernière fois chez l'oculiste, avant la guerre? (TO THE DRIVER: *Kant aysker voo zet passay poor lar dairneeair fwar shay lokilist, avan lar gayr?*)	TO THE DRIVER: La vista se l'è fatta misurare venti o cinquant'anni fa? (TO THE DRIVER: *La veesta seh leh fah-tah mee-soo-rah-reh veh-ntee oh chin-kwah-ntahn-nee fah?*)	TO THE DRIVER: ¿Cuándo le examinaron la vista? ¿Hace veinte años o cincuenta? (TO THE DRIVER: *Kwándoh leh exammináron lah beestah? Athe bénteh ányos oh thinkwéntah?*)
TO THE CONDUCTOR: Et ma monnaie, dis! (TO THE CONDUCTOR: *Ay mar mawnnay, dee!*)	TO THE CONDUCTOR: Finisca di darmi il resto, imbroglione. (TO THE CONDUCTOR: *Feenee-scah dee dah-rmee eel resto-o, eem-bro-leeoh-neh.*)	(TO THE CONDUCTOR: ¿Y dónde está la vuelta, granuja? (TO THE CONDUCTOR: *Y dóndeh stá lah bwéltah, grahnoohhah?*)
Allez embaumer quelqu'un d'autre avec vos odeurs d'ail! *(Allay ambawmay kelkan dawtr'er aveck vaw zodehr da'ee!)*	Il suo fiato puzza d'aglio. Le dispiace respirare sul viso di qualcun altro? *(Eel soo-oo fee-ah-to poo-tza d'ah-llio. Leh dees-pee-ah-cheh reh-spee-rah-reh sool vee-so dee kwal-coon ahl-tro?)*	¡Oiga! ¿Quiere echar su aliento hacia otra parte? *(Óygah! Kyéreh etchár soo ahleeyénto áthia ótrah párteh?)*

ON THE SUBWAY

Move—there's plenty of room inside.

Rücken Sie nach, da drinnen ist ja noch viel Platz.

(Rueken zee naach, daa dreennen eest jaa noach feel plaats.)

Look at those "gentlemen" hiding behind their newspapers. They're so ugly they don't want us to see them.

Sind das aber Kavaliere! Keiner steht auf und alle verstecken sich hinter ihren Zeitungen. Sie sind aber auch zu hässlich, um sich sehen zu lassen.

(Zind daas aaber cavaleere! Kyner shtayd aof oond alle fershtaykn zeesh heentr eeren tsytoongn. Zee zeend aaber aoch tsoo hayslish oom zeesh zayn tsoo laassen.)

Keep your dirty hands to yourself.

Nehmen Sie Ihre ungewaschenen Hände weg.

(Naymen zee eere oongewashenen haynde vayg.)

Stand on your own feet.

Können Sie nicht auf Ihren eigenen Füssen stehen?

(Coennen zee nisht aof eeren ygenen fuessen shtayn?)

Move over, Fatso.

Rutschen Sie mal weiter, Dicker.

(Rootshn zee maal vyter, deeker.)

Phew! Whose socks are those?

Pfui! Hier hat einer Käsefüsse.

(Phewee! heer haat yner kaysefuesse.)

FRENCH	ITALIAN	SPANISH
Poussez-vous un peu, il y a plein de place là-bas! *(Poossay-voo an pehr, eelyar pland plars lar-bar!)*	Passino avanti. C'è tanto posto laggiú. *(Pass-ee-no ah-vahn-tee. Cheh tahn-to posto lahdjew.)*	¡Quítese de en medio! ¿No ve que hay sitio? *(Keetehseh deh én médeeoh! Noh vé ké áy seettyoh?)*
Regardez donc tous ces parfaits gentlemen, tous assis derrière leur journal; avec les gueules qu'ils ont, y a pas de quoi chercher à se faire voir! (See note) *(Regarday donk too say parfay gentlemen, toos assee dereeayr lehr shoornahl; aveck lay gehrl keel zon, yar par d'kwar shairshay ass fair vwahr!)* NOTE: In France people read fewer newspapers and are less likely to hide behind them. There are very few seats on the Métro anyway: hardly anyone sits down.	Perfetti gentiluomini tutti, comodamente seduti dietro i loro giornali aperti. Forse si vergognano di far vedere i loro brutti musi. *(Per-feht-tee gen-teel-oo-oh meenee tootee, co-mo-dahmen-teh seh-doo-tee dee-ehtro ee loro joh-rnah-lee ahper-tee. For-seh see vehr-go-niah-no dee fahr vehdeh-reh ee loro broot-tee moo-see.)*	Fijáos en estos caballeros, todos sentados detrás de su periódico: son demasiado feos para enseñar la cara. *(Feehháos én éstos kabahlyéros, tóddos sentádos detráss dé soo perrióddicoh: són demmassiádoh féos párah ensenyár lah kárah.)*
Gardez vos sales pattes sur vous-même! *(Garday vaw sal pat sir voa-maim!)*	Non mi tocchi, villano *(Non mee tok-kee, villah-no.)*	¡Métase las manos en los bolsillos! *(Métaseh lás mános én lós bolseelyos!)*
Vous avez fini de me marcher dessus? *(Voo zavay feenee derm marshay dersi?)*	Ci sta bene sul mio piede? *(Chee stah beh-neh sool mee-o pee-eh-deh?)*	Aguántese usted solo, ¿quiere? *(Agooánteseh oostéh sóloh, kyéreh?)*
Hé, bouge-toi un peu, gros plein de soupe! *(Eh, boosh-twar an pehr, gro pland soop!)*	Si muova, grassone. *(See moo-o-va, grah-ssoneh.)*	¡Apártese, bola de sebo! *(Apárteseh, bólah deh séboh!)*
Pouah! Ça pue les doigts de pieds! *(Pooah! Sar pi lay dwahd peeay!)*	Che puzza! Chi è che ha paura di lavarsi i piedi? *(Keh poo-tza! Kee eh ke ah pah-oo-rah dee lah-var-see ee pee-eh-dee?)*	¡Eh! ¿De quién son estas pezuñas? *(Eh! Dé kyén són éstas pehthoonyas?)*

AT THE HOTEL

Careful with those pigskin suitcases—you should show some respect for your relatives.

Vorsichtig mit den Schweinslederkoffern! Haben Sie kein Herz für Ihre Angehörigen?

(Forzeeshteeg meet dayn shwynslaydrkoffern! haaben zee kyn, herts fuer eere aangehoerigen?)

Congratulations, your hotel has the biggest fleas in Europe.

Gratuliere! Ihr Hotel hat die grössten Flöhe Europas.

(Graatooleere! eer hotel haat dee groessten floay oyropaas.)

Congratulations, your hotel has the biggest fleas in Europe.

FRENCH

Hé, doucement avec ces valises en porc; t'as pas le respect de la famille, non?

(Eh, doosman aveck say valeez an por; tar parl respay d'lar fameey, non?)

ITALIAN

Attenzione con quelle valigie di cinghiale—non sente il richiamo del sangue?

(Atten-tzeeeoneh con kwehl- lleh vah-lee-jeh dee cheen- geah-leh—non sehn-teh eel ree-kiah-mo del sahn-goo- eh?)

SPANISH

Tenga cuidado con estas maletas de piel de cerdo, son parientes suyos.

(Téngah kwydadoh kón éstas mahlétas deh pyél deh thérdoh, sòn paryéntes soo- yos.)

Félicitations, vous avez les meilleures puces d'Europe!

(Fayleeceetasyon, voo zavay lay maiyehr pis d'Ehrop!)

Rallegramenti, il suo albergo ospita le piú grosse pulci d'Europa.

(Rah-llehgrah-mehn-tee, eel soo-oh ahl-behr-go os-pee-ta leh pew grosseh pool-chee d'Eh-oo-ro-pa.)

Le felicito: en su hotel hay las pulgas más grandes de Europa.

(Leh fehlithitoh: én soo otéll áy lás poolgas máss grándes deh Oorópah.)

33

AT THE HOTEL

How often do you hold bedbug races?

Wie oft halten Sie Wettrennen ab mit Ihrem Ungeziefer?

(Vee oft haalten zee vetrannen aap mit eerem oongetseefer?)

You even added in the date on this bill.

Sie haben ja das Datum auch mitgerechnet.

(Zee haabn yaa daas daatoom aoch mitgerayshnet.)

I suppose you were renting my room by the hour while I was out.

Sie haben wohl mein Zimmer stundenweise vermietet, während ich fort war?

(Zee haabn vohl myn tsimmr shtoondenvyze fermeetet, vairend ish fort vaar?)

Had much food poisoning here lately?

Wieviele Gäste haben Sie denn in letzter Zeit vergiftet?

(Veefeele gayste haabn zee denn in laytster tsyt fergiftet?)

I reserved a double room, not a bathroom.

Ich habe Doppelzimmer bestellt, keinen Abstellraum.

Ish haabe yn doppeltisimmer beshtellt, kynen aabshtellraom.)

I expect clean towels, not filthy rags.

Ich will saubere Handtücher haben, keine schmierigen Lappen.

(Ish vill saobre haandtuecher haabn, kyne shmeerigen laappen.)

FRENCH	ITALIAN	SPANISH
Vous organisez souvent des courses de punaises?	Per le cimici organizza gare di velocità?	¿Cuándo se organizan carreras de piojos?
(Voo zorganeezay soovan day koors der pinaiz?)	*(Per leh chee-mee-chee orga-nee-tza gah-reh dee veh-lo-chee-tà?)*	*(Kwándoh seh organnithan karréras deh peeyóhhos?)*
Vous avez même additionné la date sur cette facture!	Nel conto ha sommato anche la data?	En esta nota han sumado hasta la fecha.
(Voo zavay maim adeesyonnay lar dart sir set faktir?)	*(Nel con-to ah som-mah-to ahn-keh la da-ta?)*	*(Én éstah nótah ahn soomádoh ástah lah fétchah.)*
Je suppose que vous avez loué ma chambre à l'heure pendant mon absence?	Immagino che durante la mia assenza avrà affittato la camera a ore.	Me parece que han alquilado esta habitación mientras yo estaba fuera.
(Sher sipoawz ker voo zavay looay mar shambr ar lehr pandan mon absans?)	*(Imagin-o keh doo-rahn-teh la mee-a ah-sehn-tza ahvrah ah-feet-tah-to lah camera ah o-reh.)*	*(Meh paréthe keh ahn alkiládoh éstah abeetathión myéntras yó stábah fooérah.)*
Vous avez eu beaucoup de cas d'intoxication alimentaire, ces derniers temps?	Quanti casi di avvelenamento gastrico ci sono stati di recente?	¿No se ha intoxicado nadie con esta bazofia?
(Voo zavay zi bokood ka dantoxikarsyon aleemantair, say dairnyay tan?)	*(Kwahn-tee cah-see dee avveh - leh - nah - meh - nto gahs-tree-co chee sono stah-tee dee reh-chen-teh?)*	*(Noh seh ah intoxicádoh náddye con éstah bathóphiah?)*
J'ai demandé une chambre pour deux personnes, pas un cagibi!	Ho prenotato una camera matrimoniale, non un ripostiglio.	He reservado una habitación de matrimonio y no un cuchitril.
(Shay d'manday in shambr poor der personn, pazan casheebee!)	*(Oh preh-no-tah-to oona camera matrimonial-eh, non oon ree-post-eellio.)*	*(Eh reserbádoh oona abeetathión deh matrimónioh y noh oon kutchitrill.)*
Je veux des serviettes propres, et non pas des torchons de cuisine.	Vorrei degli asciugamani puliti, non dei cenci sporchi.	Quiero una toalla, no un trapo sucio.
(Sher vehr day serviette propr, ay non par day torshond kweezeen.)	*(Voh-ray deh-llee ah-shooga-mah-nee poo-lee-tee, non day chehn-chee s-pork-ee.)*	*(Kyéro oona toáhlya, noh oon trápoh soothyo.)*

Has anyone ever stayed here more than one night?

Ist hier etwa schon jemand länger als eine Nacht geblieben?

(Ist heer etvaa shon yaymaand laynger als yne naacht gebleeben?)

Does that smell come from your dead customers?

Hier stinkt es wie nach toten Gästen.

(Heer shtinkt es vee naach toten gaysten.)

I wanted room service, not an undertaker.

Ich habe einen Zimmerkellner gerufen, keinen Leichenbestatter.

(Ish haabe ynen tsimmerkellner geroofen, kynen lyshenbeshtaater.)

Has your laundry run out of soap? These towels are filthy!

Ihre Wäscherei hat wohl keine Seife mehr? Diese Handtücher stehen vor Dreck.

(Eere vayshery haat vohl kyne zyfe mayr? deese haantuesher shtayn for drayk.)

Did your staff escape from the insane asylum?

Besteht Ihr Personal nur aus Entlaufenen einer Irrenanstalt?

(Beshtayt eer pairzonaal noor aos entlaofenen yner irrnaanshtaalt?)

This so-called hot water is filthy and freezing.

Das heisse Wasser ist nicht nur eiskalt, sondern auch dreckig.

(Daas hysse vaasser ist nisht noor ysskaalt, zondern aoch draykig.)

FRENCH	ITALIAN	SPANISH
Vous avez parfois des clients qui restent plus d'une nuit?	Rimane mai nessuno qui piú di una notte?	¿Hay quién pase aquí más de una noche?
(Voo zavay parfwar day cleean kee rest pli din nwee?)	*(Ree-mah-neh mah-y neh-soo-no kwee pew dee oona noh-tteh?)*	*(Áy kyén páseh akkee máss deh oona nótche?)*
Dites-moi, cette odeur: ce sont vos victimes qui se décomposent?	Questo non sarà mica odore di clienti morti?	¿A qué huele aquí? ¿A clientes muertos?
(Deet-mwar, set odehr: sehr son vaw veekteem kee sehr daicompaws?)	*(Kwesto non sah-ràh mee-ka oh-do-reh dee clee-ehn-tee mohr-tee?)*	*(Ah keh welleh akee ?Ah cleeyéntes mwértos?)*
Je veux un garçon d'étage, pas un croque-mort.	Ho chiamato la cameriera, non le pompe funebri.	He pedido un camarero, no un enterrador.
(Sher vehr an garson daitash, pazan krok-mor.)	*(Oh kia-mah-to lah cah-meh-ree-ehra, non leh pom-peh foo-ne-bree.)*	*(Eh pedídoh oon kamaréroh, noh oon entehrrádór.)*
Votre blanchisserie est en grève? Ces serviettes sont sales.	È finito il sapone in lavanderia? Questi asciugamani sono luridi.	Estas toallas no han visto nunca el jabón.
(Vawtr blansheeceree ay tan graiv? Say serviette son sal.)	*(Eh fee-nee-to eel sah-po neh in lah-vahn-deh-ree-a? Kwestee ah-shoo-ga-mah-nee sonò loó-ree-dee.)*	*(Estas toáhlyas noh ahn beestoh nuunka él habón.)*
Dites-donc! Votre personnel, c'est des évadés de l'asile?	Il suo personale è composto tutto di evasi dal manicomio?	Todo su personal parece escapado de un asilo.
(Deet-donk, vawtr'er personnel, say day zaivahday d'lazeel?)	*(Eel soo-o person-ah-leh eh com-post-o toot-to dee eh-vah-see dahl mah-nee-co-mee-o?)*	*(Tawdoh soo pehrsonál pahréthe scapádoh deh oon assyloh.)*
Vous appelez ça de l'eau chaude, cette espèce de saumure glacée?	La cosiddetta acqua calda è sporca e ghiaccia.	¿A esta porquería le llaman agua caliente?
(Voo zapplay sar d'lo shawd, set espays der saumir glassay?)	*(Lah co-zi deh-ta aqua cah-ldah eh s-pork-a eh gea-chah.)*	*(Ah éstah porrkeríya leh lyáman ágwa kaleeyénteh?)*

AT THE TAILOR

I asked for a suit, not a sack.

Ich habe einen Anzug bestellt, keinen Sack.

(Ish haabe ynen aantsoog beshtaylt, kynen zaack.)

It's a perfect fit—for an elephant.

Dieser Anzug sitzt bestimmt tadellos an einem Elefanten.

(Deeser aantsoog zitst beshtimmt taadlos aan ynem elephaanten.)

Have you actually ever sold a suit before?

Haben Sie schon einen Ihrer Anzüge verkauft?

(Haabn zee shon ynen eerer aantsuege ferkaoft?)

I asked to see cloth, not tissue paper.

Ich wollte einen Anzugstoff sehen, kein Seidenpapier.

(Ish volte ynen aantsoogs-shtoff zayn, kyn zydenpaapeer.)

This suit wasn't cut; it was massacred.

Nennen Sie das Zuschneiden, was Sie da zusammengehackt haben?

(Nennen zee daas tsooshnyden, vaas zee daa tsoozaammengehaackt haaben?)

Are all your employees color-blind?

Haben Sie nur farbenblinde Gehilfen?

(Haaben zee noor faarbnblinde gehilfn?)

Do you specialize in suits for cripples?

Sie schneidern wohl hauptsächlich für Krüppel?

(Zee shnydern vol haoptzayshlish fuer krueppl?)

FRENCH	ITALIAN	SPANISH
J'ai commandé un complet, pas un sac à patates.	Le ho chiesto un abito, non un sacco.	He pedido un traje, no un saco.
(Shay commanday an complay, pazan sak ar pattat.)	*(Leh oh kee-eh-sto oon ah-beeto, non oon sah-co.)*	*(Eh pedídoh oon trahheh, nó oon sákoh.)*
Ça irait comme un gant à un éléphant.	È un taglio perfetto, per un elefante.	Las hechuras son perfectas, para un elefante.
(Sar erray kom an gan ar an elephan.)	*(Eh oon tah-llio pehr-feh-tto, per oon eh-leh-phant-eh.)*	*(Las etchooras són perfectas párah oon elephánteh.)*
C'est le premier costume que vous vendez?	Prima di oggi, lei ha mai venduto un abito?	¿Ha vendido usted alguna vez un traje?
(Sayl premier costim ker voo vanday?)	*(Pree-ma dee odjee, lay ah mah-ee ven-doo-to oon ah-beeto?)*	*(Ah bendeedoh oostéh algoonah béth oon tráhheh?)*
J'ai demandé à voir du tissu, pas du papier pelure.	Desidero vedere della stoffa, non della carta velina.	Quería ver un buen paño, no un papel higiénico.
(Shay d'manday ar vwar di teessu, par di papyay plir.)	*(Deh-see-deh-ro veh-deh-reh dehl-la stoh-ffa, non dehl-la car-ta veh-leena.)*	*(Kereeya bér oon bwén pányoh, noh oon papél eehheeyénicoh.)*
Ce costume n'as pas été coupé, on l'a taillé à coups de hâche!	Non è stato tagliato quest'abito, è stato massacrato.	Este traje no ha sido cortado, ha sido mutilado.
(Sehr costim nar par zaitay koopay, on lar tahyay ar koo der arsh!)	*(Non eh stah-to tah-lliah-to qwest'ah-beeto, eh stah-to massacr-ahto.)*	*(Esteh tráhheh nó ah seedoh cortádoh, ah seedoh mòotee-ládoh.)*
Avez-vous des employés qui sachent distinguer les couleurs?	I suoi aiutanti sono tutti orbi?	¿Es que todos sus empleados son medio ciegos?
(Avay-voo day zamplwah-yay kee sash deestangay lay koolehr?)	*(Ee soo-o-ee ah-yew-tahn-tee sono too-ttee or-bee?)*	*(Ess ké tóddos soos empleahdos són méddyo theeyégos?)*
Ainsi, vous vous spécialisez dans le vêtement pour estropiés?	Lei si specializza dunque in abiti per sciancati?	¿Sólo hacen trajes para lisiados?
(Ansee, voo voo spaysiarleezay danl vaitman poor estropeeay?)	*(Lay see speh-chahl-eetza doon-kweh in ah-beetee pehr shah-n-kah-tee?)*	*(Sóloh athen tráhhes párah leeseeyádos?)*

AT THE TAILOR

Your latest style seems to be from 1890.

Seit 1890 haben Sie wohl keine neuen Modelle mehr gehabt?

(Zyt achtsaynhoondert-noyntsig haabn zee vol kyne noyen modaylle mayr gehaabt?)

Would you believe both my legs are the same length?

Meine Beine sind gleich lang, sollten Sie wissen.

(Myne byne zind glysh laank, zolten zee vissen.)

IN THE DRESS SHOP

You must have good eyesight to be able to sew such narrow hems.

Sie müssen ja gute Augen haben, wenn Sie die winzigen Säume sehen.

(Zee muessn yaa goote aogn haaben, ven zee dee veentsign zoyme zayn.)

This is a lovely display of last year's styles.

Eine hübsche Kollektion vor-jähriger Modelle haben Sie hier.

(Yne heubshe collectsion for-yairiger modaylle haaben zee heer.)

This must be real wool—I can still smell the sheep.

Das muss ja wohl reine Wolle sein, man riecht ja noch des Schaf.

(Daas mooss yaa vol ryne volle zyn, maan reesht yaa noch daas shaaf.)

This must be silk—I can see the worm holes.

Haben die Seidenraupen diese Löcher gemacht? Dann muss es ja reine Seide sein.

(Haaben dee zydnraopen deese loysher gemaacht? daann mooss es yaa ryne zyde zyn.)

FRENCH	ITALIAN	SPANISH
Vous avez le dernier style 1890.	Sbaglio, o il suo ultimo modello risale al 1890?	Su nuevo estilo parece del año 1890.
(Voo zavayl derneeay steel deezweesan-katr'vandeece!)	*(Sbah-llio oh eel soo-oh ool-tee-mo model-oh ree-sah-leh ahl mee-lleh-ohttoh-chehn-to no-vahn-ta?)*	*(Soo nwéboh steeloh paréthe dél anyo meel otchothee-yéntos nobéntah.)*
J'ai les deux jambes pareilles, vous savez!	Le mie gambe sono tutte e due uguali, sa?	Tengo las dos piernas iguales, ¿no lo sabía?
(Shay lay dehr shamb paray, voo savay!)	*(Leh mee-eh gah-mbeh sono toot-teh eh doo-eh oo-goo-ah-lee sah?)*	*(Téngoh lás dós peeyérnas eegwáles, noh loh sabeeya?)*
Vous devez avoir la vue bien perçante pour faire des ourlets aussi minces!	Deve avere una vista perfetta chi riesce a fare un orlo con tanta poca stoffa.	Debe tener muy buena vista para hacer unos dobladillos tan estrechos.
(Voodvay zavwar lah vi byen pairsant poor fair day zoorlay aucee mans!)	*(Deh-veh ah-veh-reh oona vista pehr-feh-tta kee ree-eh-sheh ah fah-reh oon ohr-lo con tanta poca stoh-ffah.)*	*(Débeh tenér mooy bwénah beestah párah ather oonos dobladeelyos tán stretchos.)*
Quel bel étalage de modèles de l'an dernier!	Ma questa è una stupenda selezione di modelli dell'anno scorso.	Es una excelente colección de modelos pasados de moda.
(Kel bel aytahlarsh der modail der lan derneeay!)	*(Mah qwesta eh oona stoo-pendah seh-lehtzio-neh dee modeh-llee deh-ll'ah-nno scor-so.)*	*(Ess oonah excelenteh collecthion dé modélos passá-dos dé módah.)*
C'est de la vraie laine—ça sent encore le mouton!	Questa sí dev'essere lana pura—sento puzzo di pecora.	Debe ser pura lana, hasta huele a oveja.
(Say d'lar vray lane—sar san ankor l'mooton!)	*(Qwesta see deh-v'eh-sseh-reh lana poo-ra—sehn-to poo-tzo dee peh-co-rah.)*	*(Débeh sér poorah lánah, ástah wélle ah obéhhah.)*
Ça doit être de la soie—je peux encore voir les trous de vers!	Questa deve essere seta pura, è mangiata dai bachi.	Debe ser seda, veo los agujeros que hacen los gusanos.
(Sar dwar taitr d'lar swar—sher pehr ankor vwar lay trood vair!)	*(Qwesta deh-veh eh-ssehreh seh-ta poo-rah, eh mahn-jah-ta dah-y bah-kee.)*	*(Débeh sér sédah, béoh los agoohhéros ké áthen los goosános.)*

IN THE DRESS SHOP

Well, at least the label looks well made.

Na, wenigsten das Firmenschild haben Sie gut eingenäht.
(Naa, venigsten daas firmenshild haaben zee goot yngenayt.)

I asked for long sleeves, but these go down to the knees.

Gewiss, ich wollte lange Ärmel haben, aber müssen sie bis zu den Knieen reichen?
(Geviss, ish vollte laange airmel haaben, aaber muessn zee bis tsoo dayn cneen ryshen?)

Are these armholes or have the seams come apart?

Sind das die Armlöcher oder geplatzte Nähte?
(Zeend daas dee aarmloyshr oder geplaatste nayte?)

Are these armholes or have the seams come apart?

FRENCH	ITALIAN	SPANISH
Au moins, les étiquettes sont bien faites!	Be', l'etichetta è ben fatta.	Bueno, por lo menos la etiqueta parece bien cosida.
(O mwan lay zeteekett son byen fayt.)	*(Beh, l'eh-tee-keh-tta eh behn fah-ttah.*	*(Bwénoh, pór loh ménos la eteekétah paréthe byén koseedah.)*
Je voulais des manches longues, mais vous avouerez que celles-ci me descendent jusqu'aux genoux.	Volevo maniche lunghe, ma non fino al ginocchio.	Quería manga larga, pero estas me llegan hasta las rodillas.
(Sher voolay day mansh long, may vous zavooray ker selcee mer daissand shisko shernoo.)	*(Vo-leh-vo mah-nee-keh loon-geh, mah non fee-no ahl jee-nock-ee-o.)*	*(Keríya mángah lárgah, péroh éstas mé lyégan ástah las rodeelyas.)*
Dites-donc, qu'est-ce que c'est que ça? Les emmanchures ou bien les coutures qui ont foutu le camp?	Questo è il giro della manica o uno strappo nella cucitura?	¿Esto son las sobaqueras o un descosido?
(Deet-donk, kaysker say ksar? Lay zammanshir, oo byen lay kootir kee on footil kan?	*(Kwesto eh eel jee-ro deh-lla mah-nee-ca oh oono strah-ppo neh-lla coo-chee-too-ra?)*	*(Estoh són lass sawbakéras oh oon deskoseedoh?)*

IN THE DRESS SHOP

B.O.!

Schweissgeruch!
(Shvyssgerooch!)

What nice, strong stitches; do you use string, or is it rope?

Womit haben Sie diese feinen festen Stiche gemacht, Bindfaden oder einem Strick?
(Vomit haaben zee deese fynen festen shtishe gemaacht, bindfaaden oder ynem shrick?)

AT THE FISHMARKET

I'm glad to see your fish are dead, but I think they should be cremated.

Gut, dass Ihre Fische tot sind, aber Sie sollten sie lieber auch noch einäschern lassen.
(Goot, daas eere fishe tote zind, aaber zee sollten zee leeber aoch noch ynayshern laassen.)

Take your fat finger off the scales.

Nehmen Sie Ihren fetten Finger von der Waage runter.
(Naymen zee eeren fetten finger fon dair vaage roonter.)

Those aren't crabs; they're spiders.

Krabben sollen das sein? Das sind doch Spinnen.
(Craabbn zollen daas zyn? Daas zind doch shpinnen.)

FRENCH	ITALIAN	SPANISH
NOTE: There is no French equivalent of "B.O." Instead, the nose should be held between forefinger and thumb in a disdainful manner.	Che puzza di sudore! *(Keh poo-tzah dee soo-do-reh!)*	¡Huele! *(Ooéle!)*
Elles sont vachement solides, vos piqûres!—C'est de la ficelle ou de la cordelette que vous employez? *(Ell son vashman soleed, vo peekir!—Say d'lar feecelloo d'lar kordelett ker voo zamplwahyay?)*	Che bei punti; usa spago o corda? *(Keh beh-y poon-tee: oo-sa spah-go oh kor-dah?)*	¡Qué puntadas más finas! ¿Cómo las hace, con tripa o cuerda de pozo? *(Ké poontádas máss feenas! Kómoh las átheh, kón treepah oh kwérdah dé póthoh?)*
Je suis bien content de voir que vos poissons sont morts, mais vous ne pensez pas qu'il serait temps de les enterrer? *(Sher swee byen contand vwar ker vaw pwasson son mawr, may voon pansay par keel sray tan d'lay zantairay?)*	Va bene che questo pesce è morto, ma ormai dovrebbe essere anche sepolto. *(Vah beh-neh keh kwestoh peh-sheh eh mortoh, mah orma-ee dohvrehb-beh essere ankeh seh-pol-toh.)*	Me alegro de que su pescado haya muerto, ahora sólo falta que lo entierren.) *(Meh alégroh dé ké soo peskádoh áya mwértoh, aóra sóloh faltah ke loh entee-yérren.)*
Dites-donc, il faut la pousser du doigt, votre balance, pour qu'elle comprenne? *(Deet-donk, eel fo la poosay di dwar, vawtr balans, poor kel komprenn?)*	Sarebbe troppo chiederle di levare il dito dalla bilancia? *(Sah-rehbbeh troppoh kee-eh-der-leh dee leh-vah-reh eel deetoh dallah beelancha?)*	Quite el dedo de las balanzas, ¿quiere? *(Keeteh el dédoh dé las balánthas, kyéreh?)*
Eh, c'est des crabes ça, ou des araignées? *(Eh, say day crab sar, oo day zaraineeay?)*	Quelli non sono granchi, sono ragni. *(Kwellee non sonoh grankee, sono rah-nee.)*	Estos no son cangrejos, son arañas. *(Estoh noh són kangréhhos, són arányas.)*

45

AT THE FISHMARKET

Is that a codfish or one of the clerks?

Ist das ein Stockfisch oder ein Verkäufer?

(Ist daas yn shtockfish oder yn ferkoyfer?)

AT THE BUTCHER SHOP

Lamb chops? They look like dog chops to me.

Hammelkoteletts sollen das sein? Sehen ja wie Dackelkoteletts aus.

(Haammlkottletts zolln daas zyn? zayn yaa vee daacklkottletts aos.)

Do you have a foot pedal on those scales?

Können Sie die Waage auch mit den Füssen bedienen?

(Koynnen zee dee vaage aoch mit dayn fuessen bedeenen?)

This animal must have died of old age.

Das arme Tier ist wohl an Altersschwäche gestorben?

(Daas aarme teer ist vol aan aalters-shwayshe geshtorben?)

This meat is as fat as you are.

Das Fleisch ist so fett wie Sie.

(Daas flysh ist zo fett vee zee.)

Is that your hand? I thought it was old sausage.

Sind das Ihre Finger; Ich dachte, das wären fettige Würstchen.

(Zind daas eere finger? ish daachte, daas vayren fettige vuerstshen.)

FRENCH	ITALIAN	SPANISH
Dites-donc, ce merlan frit, c'est votre employé? *(Deet-donk, sehr mairlan free, say vawtr amplwah-yay?)*	Quello lí è un commesso o un baccalà? *(Kwello lee eh oon com-meh-soh oh oon bac-cah-lah?)*	¿Esto es un bacalao o el dependiente? *(Estoh éss oon bakaláoh oh él dependiyénte?)*
C'est des côtelettes d'agneau ça, ces bouts de chair flasques? *(Say day cotelait daneeo sar, say bood shair flask?)*	Quelle sarebbero cotolette d'agnello? A me sembrano di bassotto. *(Kwelleh sah-rehbbeh-roh coh-toh-leht-teh dah-nee-ehl-loh? Ah meh sembrah-noh dee bahs-soht-toh.)*	Me parece que estas chuletas son de perro, y no de cordero. *(Meh parétheh ké éstas tchoolétas són deh pérroh, ee noh dé kordéroh.)*
Vous la trafiquez du pied, cette balance? *(Voo lar trafeekay di peeay, set balans?)*	La sua bilancia funziona a pedale? *(Lah soo-ah bee-lahn-cha foon-tzee-oh-nah ah peh-dah-leh?)*	¿Tiene usted un pedal para inclinar las balanzas? *(Teeyéne oostéh oon pedál párah incleenár las balán-thas?)*
Elle est morte de vieillesse, cette bête! *(Ell ay mort der veeyeyess, set bet?)*	Quest' animale dev'essere morto di vecchiaia. *(Kwest ah-nee-mah-leh deh-vehs-seh-reh mortoh dee veh-kia-eeah.)*	Este animal debió morir de viejo. *(Esteh animál debeeyó mo-reer deh beeyéhho.)*
Elle est aussi grasse que vous, cette viande! *(Ell ay taucee grass ker voo, set veeand!)*	Questa carne è grassa come lei. *(Kwestah carneh eh grahs-sah coh-meh lay.)*	Esta carne tiene tanta grasa como usted. *(Estah kárneh teeyéne tán-tah grássah kómoh oostéh.)*
Dites-moi, ce paquet de vieilles saucisses… oh, pardon! Ce sont vos doigts! *(Deet-mwar, sparkay der veeyay saucees… oh, pardon! Sehr son vaw dwar!)*	È la sua mano quella? Credevo fossero delle salsicce. *(Eh lah soo-ah mah-noh kwellah? Creh-deh-voh foh-seh-roh deh-leh sahl-see-cheh.)*	¿Es su mano? ¡Creí que eran morcillas! *(Ess soo mánoh? Kre-ee ké éran mortheelyas!)*

47

AT THE BUTCHER SHOP

That rabbit is still meowing.

Das Kaninchen miaut ja noch.
(Daas kaaninshen meeaot yaa noch.)

AT THE GROCERY/DELICATESSEN

Cheese should have an aroma, but it shouldn't need string to tie it down.

Käse soll Aroma haben, aber keine Rollschuhe.
(Kayze zoll aaromaa haaben, aaber kyne rollshoohe.)

What grade of sand do you use in your sugar.

Mit welcher Sandsorte verfeinern Sie Ihren Zucker?
(Mit velsher zaandzorte ferfynern zee eeren tsooker?)

When you finish babbling, may I have some bacon?

Wenn Sie sich ausgeklatscht haben, geben Sie mir bitte etwas Schinken.
(Venn zee zish aosgeklaatsht haaben, gayben zee mir bitte etvaas shinken.)

Where do you dry out your used tea leaves?

Wo lassen Sie die ausgelauchten Teeblätter trocknen?
(Vo laassn zee dee aosgelaochten tayblatter troknen?)

How many times a year do you wash your hands?

Waschen Sie sich die Hände mehr als einmal im Jahr?
(Vaashen zee zish dee haynde mair aals ynmal im yaar?)

FRENCH	ITALIAN	SPANISH
Votre lapin, il miaule encore!	Quel coniglio miagola ancora?	Este conejo está maullando todavía.
(Vawtr lapan, eel meeawl ankor!)	*(Kwel coh-nee-leeoh mee-ah-goh-lah ahncorah?)*	*(Esteh konéhho stá ma-oolyandoh toddabeea.)*

| Certes, un bon fromage, ça doit sentir un peu, mais de là à le ligoter...! | Il formaggio deve, sí, avere odore, ma non deve camminare da sé. | El queso debe tener aroma, pero no debe tumbar de espaldas. |
| *(Sairt, an bon fromarsh, sar dwar santeer an pehr, may der lar al leegotay...!)* | *(Eel for-mah-jee-oh deh-veh, see, aveh-reh oh-doh-reh, mah non deh-veh cam-mee-nah-reh dah seh.)* | *(El késoh débeh tenér aró-mah, péroh noh débeh toom-bár dé espáldas.)* |

| C'est du sucre en poudre, ou du sable fin? | Che tipo di sabbia aggiunge allo zucchero che vende? | ¿Cuánta arena le pone usted al azúcar? |
| *(Say di sikran poodr, oo di sabl fan?)* | *(Keh tee-poh dee sabbeah ajewn-je alloh tzoo-keh-roh keh vehn-deh?)* | *(Kwánta arénah lé póneh oostéh al athookar?)* |

| Non, non, je vous en prie... quand vous aurez fini votre conversation, pourrais-je avoir un peu de bacon? | Quando ha finito la sua disquisizione, le dispiacerebbe darmi della pancetta? | Cuando termine de hablar, ¿me servirá un poco de jamón? |
| *(Non, non, sher voozan pree... kan voo zoray feenee vawtr convairsasyon, pooraysh avwar an pehr der barkon?)* | *(Kwandoh ah feenee-toh lah soo-ah dees-kwee-zee-tzee-oh-neh, leh dee-speea-che-reh-beh darmee dehlla pahn-chettah?)* | *(Kwándoh termeeneh dé ab-lár, meh serbeeráh oon pókoh dé hamón?)* |

| Où est-ce que vous le séchez, votre vieux marc de café? | Dove fa seccare le foglie usate del tè? | ¿Dónde pone usted a secar las hojas de té usadas? |
| *(Oo esker vool sayshay, vawtr'er vyer mar der cafay?)* | *(Doveh fa seh-kah-reh leh foh-llee-eh oo-sah-teh dehl teh?)* | *(Dóndeh póneh oostéh ah secár las ohhas dé teh oosádas?)* |

| Vos mains, vous ne les lavez qu'à la Toussaint? | Quante volte l'anno si lava le mani? | ¿Cuántas veces al año se lava las manos? |
| *(Vo man, voon lay lavay kar lar Toossan?)* | *(Kwanteh volteh lahnnoh see lah-vah leh mah-nee?)* | *(Kwántas bethes ál ányo seh lábah lás mános?)* |

AT THE GROCERY/DELICATESSEN

How many years has this salami been aging?

Wieviele Jahre ist der Lachs denn schon im Laden?

(Veefeele yaare ist dair laaks denn shon im laaden?)

Your meat pies are so full of worms, it's a wonder they don't crawl away.

Machen Ihre Fleischpasteten Wettrennen miteinander?

(Maachen eere flyshpastayten vettrennen meetynaander?)

I asked for one pound, not ten.

Ein Pfund will ich haben, nicht zehn.

(Yn pfoond vil ish haaben, nisht tsayn.)

Do you store everything in the john?

Speichern Sie Ihre Ware im Clo?

(Shpyshern zee eere vaare im clo?)

I asked for a smoked salmon, not a smoked cigar.

Geräucherten Lachs wollte ich haben, aber das ist ja Zigarrenasche, was Sie mir da geben.

(Geroysherten laaks vollte ish haaben, aaber daas ist yaa tsigarren-aashe, vaas zee mir daa gayben.)

Even my dog wouldn't eat that.

Das würde nicht 'mal mein Hund anrühren.

(Daas wuerde nisht 'maal myn hoond aanrueren.)

FRENCH	ITALIAN	SPANISH
Il est de quelle année votre salami? *(Eel ayd kel anay vawtr'er salamee?)*	Da quanti anni fa parte del suo patrimonio questo salame? *(Dah kwantee ahnee fa parteh dehl soo-oh pah-tree-moh-nee-oh kwestoh sah-lah-meh?)*	¿Cuántos años tiene esta ensaladilla? *(Kwántos ányos teeyéne éstah ensalahdeelyah?)*
Vu le nombre de vers dans vos pâtés, donnez-moi le plus rapide. *(Vi lehr nombr der vair dan vo partay, donay-mwar lehr pli rapeed.)*	Direi che potrebbe vincere una gara di velocità il suo pasticcio di carne. *(Dee-reh-ee keh po-treh-beh veen-cheh-reh oonah gah-rah dee veh-loh-chee-tah eel soo-oh pah-stee-cho dee carneh.)*	¿Sirven para medias suelas estas empanadas? *(Sirben párah méddyas swélas éstas empahnádas?)*
J'ai demandé un kilo, pas une tonne! *(Shay d'manday an keelo, pazin tonn!)*	Ne ho chiesto soltanto un chilo, non dieci. *(Neh oh kee-eh-stoh sol-tantoh oon keeloh, non dee-eh-chee.)*	Le he pedido una libra, no cuatro kilos. *(Leh eh peddeedoh oona leebrah, noh kwátro keelos.)*
Dites-donc, vous les gardez aux ouatères, vos marchandises? *(Deet-donk, voo lay garday o wahtayr, vo marshandeez?)*	Il suo deposito è in gabinetto? *(Eel soo-oh deh-poh-see-toh eh in gah-bee-neht-toh?)*	¿Lo guarda todo en el retrete? *(Loh gwárdah tódoh én él rehtréteh?)*
Je veux du saumon fumé, non du tabac dejà fumé. *(Sher vehr di sawmon fimay, non di tarbah daishar fimay.)*	Voglio del salmone affumicato, non carbonizzato. *(Voh-lleoh dehl sahl-moh-neh ah-foo-mee-cah-toh, non car-boh-nee-tzah-toh.)*	Le he pedido salmón ahumado, no ceniza de cigarrillos. *(Leh eh peddeedoh salmón aoomádoh, noh theneethah dé theegarreelyos.)*
Même mon chien n'en voudrait pas. *(Maim mon chyen nan voodray par.)*	Non la mangerebbe neppure il mio cane quella roba lì. *(Non la mahn-jeh-rehb-beh nehp-poo-reh eel mee-oh caneh kwellah roh-bah lee.)*	Ni mi perro se lo comería. *(Nee mee pérroh sé loh komereeya.)*

AT THE GROCERY/DELICATESSEN

Do you charge extra for the rust on these cans?

Der Rost an der Dose kostet wohl extra?

(Dair rost an dair doze kostet vol extraa?)

If I want yogurt, I'll ask for it. Right now I'd like some milk.

Ich sage Ihnen schon, wenn ich Yoghurt haben will, jetzt geben Sie mir Milch.

Ish zaage eenen shon, venn ish yoghurt haaben vill, yetst gayben zee mir milsh.)

Did you build your own adding machine?

Haben Sie diese Addiermaschine selbst gebastelt?

(Haaben zee deese adeermaasheene zelbst gebaastelt?)

Are these raisins or do you keep rabbits under the counter?

Sind das Sultaninen oder halten Sie Kaninchen unter dem Ladentisch?

(Zind daas zooltaneenen oder haalten zee kaaneenshen oonter daym Laadentish?)

I asked for cookies, not crumbs.

Ich habe Kekse verlangt, keine Krumen.

(Ish haabe kaykze ferlaangt, kyne kroomen.)

What a genteel way you have of picking your nose.

Sie haben eine elegante Art in der Nase zu bohren.

(Zee haaben yne elegante aart in dair naaze tsoo boren.)

FRENCH	ITALIAN	SPANISH
Vous la faites aussi payer, la rouille qu'il y a sur vos boîtes de conserves? *(Voo lar fait aucee paiyay, lar rooy keelyar sir vo bwat der consairv?)*	Fa pagare di piú per la ruggine sulle scatolette? *(Fa pah-gah-reh dee pee-oo per lah roo-jee-neh sool-leh-scah-toh-leht-tch?)*	¿Cobra aparte el orín de la lata? *(Kóbrah aparteh él oreen deh lá látah?)*
Si je veux du yaourt, je vous le dirai—pour l'instant, c'est du lait qu'il me faut. *(See sher vehr di yaoort, sher vool deeray—poor lanstan, say di lay keel mer fo.)*	Se voglio dello yoghourt glielo chiedo; adesso voglio semplicemente del latte. *(Seh voh-llee-oh dehl-loh yoh-goort llee-eh-loh kee-eh-doh; ah-dehssoh voh-llee-oh sehm-plee-cheh-menteh dehl latteh.)*	Si quiero yogurt se lo pediré. Ahora he pedido leche. *(See kyéroh yogoor sé loh peddiré. Aórah eh peddeedoh létcheh.)*
C'est votre machine à calculer? Du beau bricolage! *(Say vawtr'er masheen ar kalkilay? Di bo breekolarsh!)*	Il suo registratore di cassa se l'è costruito da sé? *(Eel soo-oh reh-jee-strah-toh-reh dee cah-sah seh leh coh-stroo-ee-toh dah seh?)*	¿Se fabrica usted mismo las máquinas de sumar? *(Sé fabrikah oostéh mees-moh lás mákeenas dé soo-mmár?)*
Dites-donc, c'est des raisins secs, ça? Ou est-ce que vous avez des lapins sous le comptoir? *(Deet-donk, say day raysan seck, sar? Oo aysker voo zavay day lahpan sool kontwar?)*	È uva passa quella, oppure tiene dei conigli sotto il banco? *(Eh oovah passah kwellah, oppooreh tee-eh-neh day-coh-nee-llee sottoh eel bancoh?)*	Aquí huele mal. ¿Es que cría conejos bajo el mostrador? *(Akee wélle mál. Ess ke kreeya konéhhos báhho él mostrádor?)*
Je veux des petits gâteaux, pas des petites miettes! *(Sher vehr day pertee garto, par day perteet myet!)*	Ho chiesto biscotti, non briciole. *(Oh kee-eh-stoh bee-scohttee, non bree-cho-leh.)*	He pedido bizcochos y no un mendrugo. *(Eh peddeedoh beethcotchos ee noh oon mendroogoh.)*
Vous avez une façon si délicate de vous fourrer le doigt dans le nez! *(Voo zavay in farson see dayleecat der voo fooray lehr dwar dan l'nay!)*	Con quale eleganza si mette le dita nel naso! *(Con kwaleh eh-leh-gantzah see meht-teh leh deetah nehl nah-soh!)*	¡Qué manera más bonita de hurgarse la nariz! *(Ké manéra máss boneetah dé oorgarseh lá nareeth!)*

AT THE GROCERY/DELICATESSEN

Do you paint your fingernails black or do you just need a bath?

Sind Ihre Fingernägel dreckig oder schwarz lackiert?

(Zind eere fingernaygel draykig oder shwarts laakeert?)

AT THE FURNITURE/DEPARTMENT STORE

What a charming pattern those scratches make.

Ein hübsches Muster haben die Schrammen da gemacht.

(Yn huebshes mooster haaben dee shraoben daa gemaacht.)

I know it has good springs—I can see half of them.

Das ist bestimmt gut gepolstert, man kann ja die Sprungfedern alle sehen.

(Daas ist beshtimmt goot gepolstert, maan kaann yaa dee shproongfaydern alle zehen.)

Are those worm holes for ventilation?

Sind das Luftlöcher oder ist hier der Holzwurm drin?

(Zind daas looftloysher oder ist heer dair holtsvoorm drin?)

Do you give prizes to people who can sleep on your beds?

Bekommt man einen Preis, wenn man auf Ihren Betten schlafen kann?

(Bekommt maan ynen price, venn maann aof eeren betten shlaafen kaann?)

FRENCH

Vous êtes en deuil ou...
c'est la couleur naturelle
de vos ongles?

*(Voo zayt zan day oo... say
lar koolehr natirel der vo
zongl?)*

ITALIAN

Le sue unghie sono a
lutto?

*(Leh soo-eh oon-ghee-eh
sonoh ah loot-toh?)*

SPANISH

¿Lleva el luto en las uñas o
es que necesita un baño?

*(Lyébah él lootoh én lás
oonyas oh éss ké netheseetah
oon banyoh?)*

Elles sont voulues, ces
égratignures?

*(Ell son vooli say zegrah-
teenyehr?)*

Che delizioso disegno
formano quelle graffiature.

*(Keh deh-lee-tzeeoso dee-
seh-neeo formah-noh kwelleh
grahf-fiah-too-reh.)*

Qué dibujo más encantador
hacen estos rasguños.

*(Ké deeboohho más enkan-
tadór áthen éstos rasgoo-
nyos.)*

Il est moelleux, c'est cer-
tain—il y a la moitié des
ressorts qui passent à tra-
vers!

*(Eel ay mwalehr, say sairtan
—eelyar lar mwatyay day
r'sawr kee pass ar trahvair!)*

Lo so che è ben molleggiato,
vedo tutte le molle.

*(Loh soh keh eh ben molleh-
jatoh, veh-doh toot-teh leh
mol-leh.)*

Sí, ya sé que es muy mu-
llido, se ven casi todos los
muelles.

*(See, yah sé ké éss mooy
moolydoh, sé vén kasee tóddos lós mwéllyes.)*

Dites-moi, ces trous de
vers, c'est pour l'aération?

*(Deet-mwar, say troo der
vair, say poor lah-airah-
syon?)*

Sono per la ventilazione
quei buchi di tarlo?

*(Soh-noh per la vehn-tee-
la-tzeeoneh kwe-ee bookee
dee tarloh?)*

¿Estos agujeros de la car-
coma, son para la ventila-
ción?

*(Estos agoohheros dé lá
karkómah, són párah lá
benteelathión?)*

Est-ce que vous récom-
pensez ceux qui arrivent
à dormir sur vos matelas?

*(Aysker voo raicompansay
sehr kee areev ar dormeer
sir vo matlar?)*

Chi riesce a dormire su
uno dei vostri letti riceve
un premio?

*(Kee ree-eh-sheh ah dor-
meereh soo oonoh day vostree
leht-tee reecheveh oon preh-
meeo?)*

¿Dan un premio a quien
consigue dormir en estas
camas?

*(Dán oon premioh a kyén
konseegue dormeer én éstas
kámas?)*

AT THE FURNITURE/DEPARTMENT STORE

I see you have handles only on some of the cups.

Ach so, nur einige Ihrer Tassen haben Henkel.

(Aach zo, noor ynige eerer taassen haaben henkel.)

What gorgeous stains on that carpet.

Himmlische Flecke sind das la auf dem Teppich.

(Himmlishe flayke zind daas daa aof dem teppish.)

Do you have a first-aid room for splinter victims?

Geben Sie bei so vielen Splittern auch 'erste Hilfe'?

(Gayben zee by zo feelen shplittern aoch 'erste hilfe'?)

When you oil chairs, you're supposed to oil the wood, not the upholstery!

Sie sollten die Stühle schmieren, nicht die Sitzflächen.

(Zee zollten dee shtuele shmeeren, nisht dee sitsflayshen.)

Do you get hairy dogs to test your chairs?

Lassen Sie Ihre Polsterstühle von langhaarigen Hunden ausprobieren?

(Laassen zee eere polster-shtuele fon laanghaarigen hoonden aosprobeeren?)

What a lovely pattern those nails make.

Ein hübsches Muster machen die Nägel da.

(Yn huebshes mooster maachen dee naygel daa.)

FRENCH	ITALIAN	SPANISH

FRENCH

Dites-moi, il faut payer un supplément pour avoir des poignées sur *toutes* les tasses?
(Deet-mwar, eel fo payay an siplayman poor avwar day pwanyay sir toot lay tass?)

ITALIAN

Vedo che solo alcune delle tazze hanno l'onore di avere un manico.
(Veh-doh keh solo alcooneh dehl-leh tah-tzeh ahnno loh-noh-reh dee avehreh oon mah-neeco.)

SPANISH

Sí, ya veo que sólo la mitad de las tazas están desportilladas.
(See, yá béoh ké sóloh lá meetád dé lás táthas stán desporteellyadas.)

Oh, la belle tâche! (Pointing towards stain on carpet.)
(Oh, lar bell tarsh!)

Che stupende macchie su quel tappeto.
(Keh stoopehn-deh makee-eh soo kwel tap-pehto.)

¡Qué mancha más decorativa tiene esta alfombra!
(Ké mántchah máss decorateebah teeyéneh ésta alfómbrah!)

Vous avez un poste de secours ici, pour les échardes qu'attrapent vos clients?
(Voo zavay an post der serkoor eecee, poor lay zeshard kattrap vo kleeyan?)

C'è un pronto soccorso per chi rimane vittima delle schegge?
(Cheh oon prontoh soccorsoh per kee reemaneh veet-teemah dehl-leh skeh-jeh?)

¿Disponen de botiquín para quitar las astillas que uno se clava?
(Deespónen dé boteekeen párah keetár lás asteellyas ké oonoh sé clábah?)

Pour être huilées, elles le sont vos chaises. Il y en a partout.
(Poor aytr weelay, ell lehr son, vo shaiz. Eel yana partoo.)

Quando si dà l'olio alle seggiole non c'è bisogno di metterlo sui sedili.
(Kwando see dah loh-leeo alleh seh-joh-leh non cheh beeso-neeo dee mehtterloh soo-ee seh-dee-lee.)

Al engrasar los sillones, ponga el aceite en las ruedas, no en la tapicería.
(Al engrasár lós seellyónes, póngah él athéyteh én lás rooédas, noh én lah tapeetherea.)

Dites-donc, ces fauteuils, ce sont les singes qui les essayent qui y laissent tous leurs poils?
(Deet-donk, say fawtay, sehr son lay sansh kee lay zessay kee ee laiss too lehr pwal?)

Le vostre sedie vengono collaudate da cani che perdono il pelo?
(Leh vostreh seh-dee-eh vengonoh cohllah-oo-dah-teh dah cah-nee keh perdoh-noh eel peh-loh?)

¿Tiene usted perros rabiosos para probar su sillería?
(Teeyéne oostéh pérros rrabeeyósos párah probár soo seellyerea?)

Eh, voilà un bel arrangement de clous!
(Eh, vwalar an bel aranshman der cloo!)

Come sono disposti artisticamente quei chiodi!
(Coh-meh sono dee-spohstee artee-stee-cah-mehn-teh kwe-ee kee-oh-dee!)

¡Qué arabesco más bonito forman estos arañazos!
(Ké arabéskos máss boneetos fórman éstos aranyathos!)

57

AT THE SHOE STORE

I expect your shoes to fit my feet, not my feet to fit your shoes.

Ihre Schuhe sollen meinen Füssen passen, nicht meine Füsse Ihren Schuhen.

(Eere shoohe zollen mynen fuessen paassen, neesht myne fuesse eeren shoohen.)

What lovely antique styles you have.

Sie haben so hübsche antiquarische Modelle.

(Zee haaben zo huebshe antiqvaarishe modaylle.)

I asked for walking shoes, not dancing slippers.

Warum zeigen Sie mir Abendschuhe, wenn ich Strassenschuhe haben will?

(Vaaroom stygen zee mir aabendshoohe, venn ish shtraassenshoohe haaben vill?)

These shoes stink.

Diese Schuhe stinken.
(Deese shoohe shtinken.)

These fit fine—they feel just like a tourniquet.

Diese sitzen sehr gut—wie ein Schraubstock.

(Deese zitsen zayr good—vee yn shraob-shtock.)

I wasn't a cripple when I came in and I don't want to be a cripple when I go out.

Ich war kein Krüppel, als ich hier reinkam und ich will auch kein Krüppel sein, wenn ich hier rausgehe.

(Ish vaar kyn crueppel, aals ish heer rynkaam oond ish vill aoch kyn crueppel zyn, venn ish heer raosgayhe.)

FRENCH	ITALIAN	SPANISH
C'est à vos chaussures de convenir à mon pied, et non pas le contraire!	Sono le scarpe che devono andare bene ai piedi, non i piedi alle scarpe.	Espero que sus zapatos se adapten a mis pies, y no mis pies a sus zapatos.
(Saytar vo shawssir der convneer ar mon peeay, ay non parl contrair!)	*(Soh-noh leh scar-peh keh deh-voh-noh ahndar beh-neĥ ah-ee pee-eh-dee, non i pee-eh-dee alleh scar-peh.)*	*(Spéroh ké soos thapátos sé adápten ah mees pyés ee no mees pyés ah soos thapátos.)*
Oh, les belles chaussures à l'ancienne mode que vous vendez!	Che bei modelli stile antico che avete.	¡Qué bellos modelos para un anticuario!
(Oh, lay bell shawssir ar lansyen mod ker voo vanday!)	*(Keh beh-ee moh-deh-lee stee-leh antee-coh keh ah-veh-teh.)*	*(Ké béllyos modélos párah oon antikwareeyo!)*
J'ai dit des chaussures de marche, pas des escarpins pour aller au bal.	Voglio delle scarpe da passeggio non da ballo.	Quiero unos zapatos de calle, no unas zapatillas de ballet.
(Shay dee day shawssir der marsh, par day zescarpan poor allay o bahl!)	*(Voh-llee-oh dehl-leh scar-peh dah pahs-seh-joh non da bahl-loh.)*	*(Kyéro oonos thapátos dé kállye, noh oonas thapateellyas deh ballyét.)*
Elles puent, ces tatanes!	Queste scarpe puzzano.	Estos zapatos huelen a queso.
(Ell pi, say tatarn!)	*(Kweh-steh scar-peh poo-tzah-noh.)*	*(Estos thapátos wellen ah késoh.)*
Elles serrent à merveille ces chaussures, on dirait un étau!	Queste scarpe fasciano benissimo, anzi fermano la circolazione.	Sí, me caen tan bien como un torniquete.
(Ell sair tar mairvay say shawssir, on deeray anai-taw!)	*(Kweh-steh scar-peh fah-shah-no beh-nees-eemo, ahn-tzee fehrmahno la cheer-coh-lah-tzeeoneh.)*	*(See, meh káen tán byén cómoh oon tornikéteh.)*
Je n'étais pas estropié en entrant dans votre magasin, et je ne tiens pas à l'être quand j'en sortirai.	Non ero zoppo quando sono entrato e non voglio essere zoppo quando esco.	No estaba cojo cuando he venido y no quiero estarlo cuando me marche.
(Sher naitay par zestropeeay an antran dan vaw-tr'er magazan, ay shern tyen par zar laytr'er kan shan sorteeray.)	*(Non eh-roh tzohp-poh kwando sono ehntrahtoh eh non voh-llee-oh ehssehreh tzohp-poh kwando eh-scoh.)*	*(No stábah cóhho kwándo é behneedoh ee noh kyéroh stárloh kwándoh meh már-cheh.)*

AT THE SHOE STORE

Where do you buy *your* shoes?

Und wo kaufen Sie Ihre eigenen Schuhe?

(Oond vo kaofen zee eere ygenen shoohe?)

I asked for a salesclerk, not a blacksmith.

Ich will Schuhe haben, keinen Hufbeschlag.

(Ish vill shoohe haaben, kynen hoof-beshlaag.)

What wonderful things they do with cardboard these days.

Was heute nicht alles mit Pappe gemacht werden kann.

(Vaas hoyte nisht aalles meet paappe gemaacht wayrden kaann.)

You fool, I don't have two left feet.

Glauben, Sie, ich habe zwei linke Füsse, Sie Trottel?

(Glaoben zee, ish haabe tsvy linke fuesse, zee trottl?)

AT THE RESTAURANT/CAFÉ

How many times have you reheated this meal?

Wie oft haben Sie dieses Essen schon aufgewärmt?

(Vee oft haabn zee deeses ayssen shon aofgevayrmt?)

Do you run your own hospital for people who eat here?

Bringen Sie die Leute, die hier essen, in Ihrem Privatkranken-haus unter?

(Breengn zee dee loyte, dee heer ayssen, in eerem prevaatcraanknhaos oonter?

FRENCH	ITALIAN	SPANISH

Où est-ce que vous vous chaussez, vous-même?

(Oo aysker voo voo shawssay voo-maim?)

E lei da che calzolaio si serve?

(Eh lay dah keh cal-tzoh-lah-eeo see sehrveh?)

¿Dónde compra usted su calzado?

(Dóndeh kómprah oostéh soo kalthádoh?)

TO THE FITTER: Dites-donc, vous êtes forgeron de votre métier?

(TO THE FITTER: *Deet-donk, voo zayt forsheron d'vawtr maityay?)*

Desideravo un calzolaio non un fabbro ferraio.

(Deh-see-deh-rah-voh oon cal-tzoh-lah-eeo non oon fahb-broh fehr-rah-eeo.)

Buscaba un zapatero, no un herrador.

(Booskábah oon thapatéroh, noh oon erradór.)

Ah le progrès! Je n'ai jamais vu de carton d'aussi belle qualité!

(Ah ler progray! Shnay jahmay vi der karton daucee bell kahleetay!)

Certo che oggigiorno fabbricano un cartone stupendo.

(Chehrto keh oh-jee-johr-noh fahb-bree-cah-no oon cartohneh stoopehndo.)

¡Qué bonitos zapatos, si no fueran de cartón!

(Ké boneetos thapátos, see noh fwéran dé cartón!)

Dites-donc, j'ai aussi un pied droit comme tout le monde!

(Deet-donk, shay aucee an peeay drwar, komm tool mond!)

Imbecille, non ho due piedi sinistri.

(Eembeh-chee-leh, non oh doo-eh pee-eh-dee see-nee-stree.)

¡No tengo dos pies izquierdos, animal!

(Noh tengoh dós peeyés eethkeeyerdos, animál!)

Combien de fois vous l'avez déjà réchauffé, ce plat?

(Kombyen der fwar voo lavay dayshar reshawfay, sehr plar?)

Quante volte è stata riscaldata questa pietanza?

(Kwanteh vohl-teh eh stah-tah rees-cahl-dah-tah kweh-stah pee-eh-tahn-zah?)

¿Cuántas veces ha recalentado este plato?

(Kwántas béthes ah rrecalentádoh esteh plátoh?)

Vous avez votre propre clinique, j'espère, pour ceux qui mangent chez vous?

(Voo zavay vawtr'er propr'er kleeneek, shaispair, poor sehr kee mansh shay voo?)

Per la gente che mangia qui, c'è un ospedale speciale?

(Per lah jehn-teh keh mahn-jah kwee cheh oon oh-speh-dah-leh speh-chah-leh?)

¿Tienen un hospital para los que comen aquí?

(Teeyénen oon ospitál párah loss ké cómen akee?)

61

AT THE RESTAURANT/CAFÉ

Is there a recipe for this or did it just accumulate from leftovers?

Gibt es ein Rezept für dieses Essen oder hat es sich aus Resten von selbst gekocht?

(Geebt es yn recept fuer deeses ayssen oder haat es seesh aos rayston fon zelbst gecocht?)

This is the best water soup I've ever tasted.

Habe noch nie solche gute Wassersuppe gegessen.

(Haabe noch nee zolshe goote vasserzooppe gegayssen.)

Is this supposed to be veal or tripe?

Ist das Kalbfleisch oder Eingeweide?

(Eest das caalbflysh oder yngevyde?)

Get your dirty thumb out of the soup.

Nehmen Sie Ihren dreckigen Daumen aus meiner Suppe.

(Naymen zee eeren draykeegen daomen aos myner zooppe.)

Did the cook take a bath in this soup?

Der Koch hat wohl erst in der Suppe gebadet?

(Dair coch haat vol airst in dair zooppe gebaadet?)

Has the electricity been cut off? I asked for a hot meal.

Hatten Sie hier Kurzschluss? Das Essen ist ja ganz kalt.

(Haatten zee heer koorts-shlooss? Daass ayssen eest ja gants cult.)

FRENCH	ITALIAN	SPANISH

Dites-donc, vous l'avez fait à partir d'une recette, ou bien vous avez simplement accomodé les restes?

(Deet-donk, voo lavay fay ar parteer din rehsett, oo byen voo zavay sanplerman arkomoday lay rest?)

Questo piatto è cucinato secondo una ricetta o sono degli avanzi messi insieme?

(Kweh-sto pee-ah-tto eh coo-chee-nah-toh secondoh oonah ree-cheht-tah oh sono deh-llee ah-vahn-tzee mehs-see een-see-eh-meh?)

¿Este plato lo hacen con receta, o con las sobras de los demás?

(Esteh plátoh loh áthen cón rrethétah oh cón lass sóbras dé tóddos loss dehmáss?)

C'est le meilleur bouillon d'eau que j'aie jamais goûté!

(Sayl maiyehr booyon do ker shay sharmay gootay!)

Questa è la migliore mine-stra all'acqua che abbia mai gustato.

(Kwehsta èh lah mee-lleeo-reh mee-neh-stra allahk-kwa keh ahb-beeah mah-ee goostah-toh.)

Es la mejor sopa de agua que he probado.

(Ess lá mehhór sópah dé ágwa ké eh probádoh.)

Dites-donc, c'est du veau ou de la tripe?

(Deet-donc, say di vo oo d'lar treep?)

Dovrebbe essere vitella o trippa questa?

(Dovrehb-beh ehs-seh-reh vee-tehlla oh treep-pa kweh-sta?)

¿Esto es ternera o una piltrafa?

(Estoh éss ternérah oh oonah peeltráfah?)

Sortez-moi ce gros pouce de ma soupe!

(Sortay-mwar sehr gro poos d'mar soop!)

Tolga il suo sudicio dito dalla minestra.

(Tohlga eel soo-oh soo-dee-cho deetoh dahl-lah mee-neh-stra.)

Saque el dedo gordo de la sopa.

(Sákeh él dédoh górdoh dé lá sópah.)

Pouah! Ça de la soupe? On dirait que le chef s'est lavé les pieds là-dedans!

(Pouah! Sar d'lar soop? On deeray klehr chef say larvay lay peeay lard-dan!)

In questa minestra ha fatto il bagno il cuoco?

(Een kwehsta mee-neh-stra ah fattoh eel bah-neeoh eel kwocoh?)

¿Se ha bañado el cocinero en esta sopa?

(Seh ah banyádoh él cothee-néroh én éstah sópah?)

Vous n'avez plus de feu? J'ai demandé un plat chaud.

(Voo navay plid fehr? Shay d'manday an piar shaw.)

È mancata la corrente? Io volevo un pasto caldo.

(Eh mahn-cah-ta lah cor-rehn-teh? Eeo vohlehvo oon pah-stoh cahldoh.)

¿Les han cortado la luz? He pedido un plato caliente.

(Lés án cortádoh lah looth? Eh peddeedoh oon plátoh caleeyénteh.)

Does a magnifying glass come with the meal?

Gehört zu dem Essen nicht auch ein Vergrösserungsglas?

(Ge-hurt tsoo daym ayssen nisht aoch yn fergroesseroongs-glaace?)

I'm sorry to learn that all your waiters died.

Es tut mir leid, zu hören, dass Ihre Kellner alle gestorben sind.

(Es toot meer lyd tsoo hoeren daass eere kayllner aalle geshtorben zeend.)

Are your tables designed for skinny people?

Haben Sie nur Tische für dünne Gäste?

(Haaben zee noor tishe fuer duenne gayste?)

Did this meat come from a tannery?

Kommt dieses Fleisch aus einer Lederfabrik?

(Commt deezes flysh aos yner layderfaabreek?)

I asked for rare, not raw.

Innen rot sollte das Fleisch sein, nicht aussen roh.

(Innen roat zollte daass flysh zyn, neesht aossen row.)

Is this a vegetarian restaurant—or am I supposed to believe that this is meat?

Soll das kleine Stück hier Fleisch sein, oder bin ich in einem vegetarischen Restaurant?

(Zoll daass clyne shtuek heer flysh zyn, oder bin eesh in ynem vayg-ey-taarishen restorong?)

FRENCH	ITALIAN	SPANISH
Il me faut une loupe pour trouver ce que vous me servez!	Con i suoi pasti dà anche una lente di ingradimento?	¿No dan una lupa, junto con la comida?
(Eel mehr fo tin loop poor troovay sker voom sairvay!)	*(Cohn ee soo-oh-ee pah-stee dah ahn-keh oona lehn-teh dee eengrandeemehntoh?)*	*(Noh dán oonah loopah, hoontoh cón lá comeedah?)*
Ils sont tous morts, vos garçons?	Quanto mi addolora constatare che sono morti tutti i camerieri.	Es una lástima que todos los camareros se hayan muerto.
(Eel son toos mawr, vo garson?)	*(Kwantoh mee ahd-doh-lo-hra cohn-stahtah-reh keh sohnoh mortee toot-tee ee cameree-eh-ree.)*	*(Ess oona lásteemah ké tóddos lóss kamahréros sé áyan mwértoh.)*
Vous n'avez que des tables pour gringalets?	Le sue tavole sono esclusivamente per gente magra?	¿Estas mesas son para personas delgadas?
(Voo navay ker day tarbl'er poor grangalay?)	*(Leh soo-eh tah-voh-leh sohnoh eh-scloo-see-vah-mehnteh per jehn-teh mah-gra?)*	*(Estas mésas són párah persónas delgádas?)*
Vous l'achetez à la tannerie, votre viande?	Questa carne l'ha acquistata alla conceria?	¿Esta carne la sirven en la fábrica de cueros?
(Voo lashtay ar lar tanree, vawtr'er veeand?)	*(Kweh-sta carneh lah ak-kwee-stah-ta ahl-la cohn-cheh-reeah?)*	*(Esta cárneh lá seerben én lá fábreeka dé kwéros?)*
J'ai dit saignant, pas cru!	L'ho chiesta al sangue, non cruda.	He pedido que estuviera poco hecha, no cruda del todo.
(Shay dee sainyan, par cri!)	*(Loh kee-eh-stah ahl sahngoo-eh, non crooda.)*	*(Eh peddeedoh ké stoobee-yérah pókoh etchah, noh croodah dél tódoh.)*
C'est de la viande, ce machin, ou vous ne servez que des végétariens?	Non sapevo che questo fosse un ristorante vegetariano—o quello lo chiama un pezzo di carne?	¿Es un restaurante vegetariano o quiere hacerme creer que esto es carne?
(Say d'lar veeand, sehr marshan, oo voon sairvay ker day vaishaitahryan?)	*(Non sah-peh-voh keh kwehsto fosseh oon ree-stohrahn-teh veh-jeh-tah-reeahno—oh kwello loh kiamah oon peh-tzoh dee carneh?)*	*(Ess oon restaooránteh behetareeánoh oh kyére athérme kré-ér ké ésto ess cárneh?)*

AT THE RESTAURANT/CAFÉ

That fly looks extremely well done.

Diese Fliege haben Sie sehr gut gekocht.

(Deese fleege haaben zee zair goot gaycocht.)

How many people chewed this before I got it?

Haben hier schon viele Leute vorher dran rumgekaut?

(Haaben heer shon feele loyte forhair dran room-ge-caot?)

Do you kill your own cabbage here?

Schlachten Sie auch Ihren eigenen Kohl?

(Shlaachten zee aoch eeren ygenen coal?)

Do you serve bicarbonate with every course?

Geben Sie zu jedem Gang Verdauungstabletten?

(Gayben zee tsoo jaydem gaang ferdow-oongs-taabletten?)

Shaking that bottle won't make it a sparkling wine.

Schütteln Sie den Wein, damit Champagner draus wird?

(Shuettln zee dayn vyn, daameet champaanier draos veerd?)

This tablecloth is filthy. Did it come right off your bed?

Das Tischtuch ist dreckig. Wurde es schon als Bettuch benutzt?

(Daass tishtooch eest draykeeg. voorde ays shon aals bet-tooch benootst?)

Sure you deserve a tip—the tip of my boot.

Trinkgeld erwarten Sie? Einen Tritt können Sie haben.

(Tringk-gayld ervaarten zee? yner tritt koennen zee haaben.)

FRENCH	ITALIAN	SPANISH
Oh la belle mouche! C'qu'elle est bien cuite! *(Oh lar bell moosh! Skel ay byen cweet!)*	Quella mosca è cotta alla perfezione. *(Kwella moh-ska eh cottah ahl-la per-feh-tzeeoh-neh.)*	Esta mosca está muy bien guisada. *(Éstah móskah stá mooy beeyén geesádah.)*
Vous l'avez donné à mâcher à tout le monde, avant de me servir? *(Voo lahvay donnay ar marshay ar tool mond, ahvan d'mer sairveer?)*	Questo, quanta gente lo ha già masticato? *(Kweh-stoh, kwanta jehn-teh loh ah jah mah-stee-cah-toh?)*	¿Cuántos clientes lo han masticado antes que yo? *(Kwántos cleeyéntes loh án masteekádoh ántess ké yó?)*
Mais ils sont vivants, vos choux! *(May zeel son veevan, vo shoo!)*	I vostri cavoli vengono uccisi a tavola? *(Ee voh-stree cah-voh-lee vehn-goh-noh ooocheesee ah tah-voh-lah?)*	¿Mata usted mismo aquí sus verduras? *(Mátah oostéh meesmoh akee soos berdooras?)*
Vous devriez servir entre chaque plat des pilules contre les maux d'estomac. *(Voo dehvreeay sairveer an-tr'er shack plar day peelil contr'er lay maw daistomar.)*	Con ogni portata servite anche delle pasticche digestive? *(Cohn oh-nee portah-ta sehr-vee-teh an-keh dehl-leh pah-steeckeh deejeh-stee-veh?)*	¿Sirven pastillas digestivas con cada comida? *(Seerben pasteellyas dihhestivas cón cáddah comeedah?)*
Vous avez fini de maltraiter cette bouteille, c'est pas du mousseux que je veux! *(Voo zavay feenee d'maltraitay set bootay, say par di moosehr kersh ver!)*	Sta scuotendo quel vino per farne dello spumante? *(Stah skwo-tehndoh kwel vee-noh per farneh dehl-loh spoomanteh?)*	¿Agita usted el vino para que parezca espumoso? *(Aheetah oostéh meesmoh él beenoh párah ké paréthka spoomósoh?)*
La nappe est dégueulasse! On y a couché dessus? *(Lar nap ay daigehrlass! On ee ar kooshay d'si?)*	Questa tovaglia è schifosa— è già stata usata come lenzuolo? *(Kweh-sta toh-vah-lleea eh skee-foh-sa—eh stah-tah jah oosah-tah coh-meh lehn-tzoo-oh-lo?)*	Este mantel es un asco ¿es una sábana sucia? *(Esteh mantél éss oon áskoh éss oona sábanah sootheeya?)*
Comment, un pourboire? Allez vous faire voir! *(Koman, an poorbwar? Allay voo fair vwar!)*	Altro che mancia, un calcio si merita. *(Ahl-troh keh manchah, oon cahl-cho see meh-ree-ta.)*	Se merece una patada de propina. *(Seh meréthe oona patádah dé propeenah.)*

When I want a cold meal, I'll ask for one.

Wenn ich ein kaltes Essen haben will, werde ich es sagen.

(Vaynn eesh yn kaaltes ayssen haaben veell, vairde eesh ays saagen.)

I asked for olive oil, not motor oil.

Ich wollte Olivenöl haben, kein Schmieröl.

(Ish vollte oleeven-oel haaben, kyn shmeer-oel.)

I asked for olive oil, not motor oil.

Je vous le dirai, lorsque je voudrais manger froid!

(Sher vool deeray, lorsker sher voôdray manshay frwar!)

Se voglio un pasto freddo di solito lo ordino.

(Seh voh-lleeoh oon pah-stoh frehd-hoh dee soh-lee-toh loh or-dee-noh.)

Cuando quiera un plato frío se lo pediré.

(Kwándoh kyérah oon plá-toh freeoh seh loh pedeeréh.)

J'ai demandé de l'huile d'olive, pas de moteur!

(Shay d'manday der l'weel doleev, pard motehr!)

Ho chiesto olio da condire, non da macchina.

(Oh kee-eh-stoh oh-lleeo dah con-dee-reh, non dah mahk-kee-nah.)

Le he pedido aceite de oliva, no aceite para mo-tores.

(Leh eh peddedoh athéyteh dé oleebah, noh athéyteh párah motóres.)

AT THE RESTAURANT/CAFÉ

When did the waiters go on strike?

Wie lange streiken Ihre Kellner schon?

(Vee laange shtryken eere kayllner shon?)

Now get someone who knows how to add to total up the bill.

Den Rechenkünstler möchte ich sehen, der diese Rechnung auf die gleiche Endsumme bringt.

(Dayn rayshen-kuenstler moeshte eesh zayn, dair deeze raysh-noong aof dee glyshe end-zoomm breenkt.)

Why don't you hire a chef to do the cooking instead of a dishwasher?

Sie sollten einen Küchenchef engagieren und das Essen nicht von einem Kuli kochen lassen.

(Zee zollten ynen kueshen-chef aang-aajeeren oond daass ayssen neesht fon ynem koolee cochen laassen.)

This soup looks like dishwater.

Ist das Suppe oder Abwaschwasser?

(Eest daass zooppe oder aabwaashvaasser?)

That's not the bill—it's the National Debt.

Das ist keine Rechnung, das ist eine Aufstellung für den Staatshaushalt.

(Daass eest kyne rayshnoong, daas eest yne aofshtelloong fuer dayn shtaats-haos-haalt.)

Do any customers ever come back?

Ist schon einer Ihrer Kunden wiedergekommen?

(Eest shon yner eerer koonden veeder-gecommen?)

I asked for it roasted, not incinerated.

Braten sollten Sie das Fleisch, nicht einäschern.

(Braaten zollten zee daass flysh, neesht yn-ayshern.)

FRENCH	ITALIAN	SPANISH
Depuis quand sont-ils en grève, vos garçons? *(Derpwee kan sonteel an graiv, vo garson?)*	Quando sono scesi in sciopero i camerieri? *(Kwando sono sheh-zee een sho-peh-roh ee cah-meh-ree-eh-ree?)*	¿Cuándo empezó la huelga de camareros? *(Kwándo empethó lá wéllgah dé camahréros?)*
Maintenant, allez me chercher quelqu'un qui sache faire proprement une addition. *(Mantnan, allœym shairshay kelkan kee sash fair proprerman in adeesyon.)*	Ed ora chiami qualcuno che il conto lo sa fare. *(Ehd oh-rah kiamee kwalcoono keh eel cohn-to loh sah fareh.)*	¿No hay nadie que sepa sumar la nota? *(Nó áy nádeeye ké sépah soomár lá nótah?)*
Et si vous employiez un chef, plutôt qu'un plongeur, pour faire votre cuisine? *(Eh see voo zamplwayay an chef, plitaw kan plonshehr, poor fair vawtr cweezeen?)*	Perché non impiega un cuoco per cucinare invece di uno sguattero? *(Per-keh non eem-pee-eh-ga oon kwoco per coo-chee-nareh een-veh-cheh dee oonoh sgoo-aht-teh-ro?)*	¿Por qué no alquilan un cocinero en lugar de un pinche para hacer la comida? *(Pór ké noh alkeelan oon cotheenéroh én loogar dé oon peencheh párah athér lá comeedah?)*
Ce n'est pas de la soupe, c'est de l'eau de vaisselle! *(Snay par d'lar soop, say d'lawd vaisell!)*	Questa minestra sembra l'acqua del rigovernato. *(Kweh-sta mee-neh-stra sehm-bra lahk-kwa dehl reego-vehr-nahto.)*	Esta sopa está hecha con el agua de lavar los platos. *(Estah sópah stá etchah cón él ágwa dé lavár loss plátos.)*
Vous appelez ça l'addition? —C'est un budget d'état! *(Voo zapplay sar ladeesyon? —Say tan bidjay daytar!)*	Quello non è un conto, è un bilancio nazionale. *(Kwello non eh oon cohntoh, eh oon bee-lancho nah-tzeeo-naleh.)*	Esto no es la nota, es el Presupuesto Nacional. *(Estoh nó éss lá sópah, éss él Prehsoopwéstoh Nathionál.)*
Vous avez des clients qui reviennent manger ici? *(Voo zavay day cleeyan keer vyen manshay eecee?)*	Capita mai che un cliente torni una seconda volta? *(Cah-pee-ta mah-ee keh oon clee-ehn-teh tornee oona sehconda volta?)*	¿Hay algún cliente que vuelva por segunda vez? *(Ay algoon cleeyénteh ké bwélbah pór segoondah béth?)*
J'ai dit rôti, pas carbonisé! *(Shay dee rawtee, par carboneezay!)*	Lo volevo arrosto non incenerito. *(Loh volehvoh ar-roh-stoh non een-che-nehree-to.)*	Lo quería asado, no carbonizado. *(Loh kereeya assádoh, nó carbonithádoh.)*

Frozen food should be defrosted before serving.

Tiefgefrorenes müssen Sie aber vor dem Servieren auftauen.
(Teef-gefrorenes muessen zee aaber for daym zerveeren aoftao-n.)

What lovely patterns those grease stains make on your shirt.

Die Fettflecke auf Ihrem Hemd bilden aber ein hübsches Muster.
(Dee faytt-flayke aof eerem haymd beelden aaber yn hueb-shes mooster.)

Will you please spit all over somebody else?

Können Sie nicht in eine andere Richtung spucken?
(Koennen zee neesht in yne aandere rish-toong shpookken?)

I asked for crêpe suzette, not crêpe paper.

Crêpe suzette wollte ich haben, kein Krepp-Papier.
(Crepe suzette vollte eesh haaben, kyn kraypp-paapeer.)

I asked for pancakes, not cow flop.

Pfannen-Kuchen wollte ich haben, keine Kuh-Fladen.
(Pfaannen-koochen vollte eesh haaben, keine koo-flaaden.)

I wanted a cigar, not a twig.

Was bringen Sie mir so ein spindeldürres Ding—ich habe doch eine Zigarre verlangt.
(Vaas breengen zee meer zo yn shpindl-duerres deengk—eesh haabe doch yne tseegaarre ferlaangt.)

FRENCH	ITALIAN	SPANISH

Je vois qué vous n'avez pas eu le temps de dégivrer cette nourriture.

(Sher vwar ker voo navay par zil tan der daisheevray set nooreetir.)

Prima di servire i cibi surgelati bisogna sghi acciarli.

(Preema dee serveereh ee chee-bee soor-jeh-lah-tee bee-zoh-nia sghee-ah-charlee.)

Los alimentos congelados hay que descongelarlos antes de servir.

(Loss aleementos conhhéláh-dos áy ké desconhhelárlos ántess dé serbeer.)

On voit que vous employez du vrai beurre à en juger par ces belles tâches qui ornent votre plastron!

(On vwar ker voo zamplwayay di vray behr, ar an shishay pahr say bell tarsh kee orn'er vawtr'er plahstron!)

Quelle macchie unte sulla sua camicia stanno proprio bene.

(Kwelleh mak-kee-eh oonteh soolla soo-ah cah-mee-ceeah stannoh proh-preeoh behneh.)

Estas manchas de grasa en la camisa son muy decorativas.

(Estas mántchas dé grássa én lá cameesah són mooy decorativas.)

Postillonnez ailleurs, je n'ai pas mon parapluie aujourd'hui.

(Posteeyon ahyehr, shnay par mon paraplwee aushoordwee!)

Le dispiacerebbe sputare su qualcun altro?

(Leh dee-spee-ah-cheh-rehb-beh spootareh soo kwalcoon ahltroh?)

Vaya usted a escupir a otra parte.

(Báyah oostéh ah eskoopeer ah ótrah párteh.)

J'ai demandé une crêpe suzette, pas du papier gaufré.

(Shay d'manday in crape sizet, par di papyay gofray.)

Ho chiesto crêpes suzette non carta increspata.

(Oh kee-eh-sto crehp sooseht non carta een-creh-spahta.)

He pedido patatas crêpe, no papel de seda.

(Eh peddeedoh patátas crép, noh papél dé sédah.)

J'ai demandé une crêpe, pas une crotte!

(Shay d'manday in crape, pazin crott!)

Ho chiesto delle fritelle non delle suole da scarpa.

(Oh kee-eh-sto dehl-leh freetehl-leh non dehl-leh soo-oh-·leh da scarpah.)

He pedido frutas de sartén, no boñigas de buey.

(Eh peddeedoh frootas dé sartén, noh bawnygas deh bwéy.)

Je voulais un cigare, pas une branche d'arbre!

(Sher voolay an seegar, pazin bransh d'arbr.)

Volevo un sigaro non un rametto secco.

(Voh-leh-vo oon see-gah-ro nohn oon rah-meht-toh sehk-ko.)

Quiero un cigarro, no un tronco.

(Kyéroh oon thigarroh, noh oon tróncoh.)

AT THE RESTAURANT/CAFÉ

This isn't wine; it's vinegar.

Das ist Essig, kein Wein.
(Daas eest ayssig, kyn vyn.)

I asked for wine, not cork soup.

Ich habe Wein bestellt und keine Korksosse.
(Eesh haabe vyn beshtayllt oond kyne cork-zosse.)

Was this omelet made with dinosaur eggs?

Das Omelett wurde wohl mit Eiern von vorsintflutlichen Reptilien gemacht?
(Daass omelette voorde vol meet y-ern fon for-sintflootlishn rayptilian ge-maacht?)

May I have a separate plate for the maggots?

Bringen Sie mir doch noch bitte einen Teller für die Maden.
(Breengn zee meer doch noch bitte y-nen tayller fuer dee maaden.)

Are the coats in the cloakroom for sale?

Sie verkaufen wohl die besten Mäntel in der Garderobe?
(Zee ferkaofen vol dee baysten mayntel in der Gar-de-robe?)

AT THE THEATER

Can't you read a ticket? That seat's mine.

Können Sie nicht lesen? Das ist mein Sitz.
(Koennen zee nisht laysn? daass eest myn zits.)

FRENCH	ITALIAN	SPANISH

C'est du vinaigre, votre vin!
(Say di veenaigr'er vawtr van!)

Questo vino è aceto.
(Kweh-stoh veenoh eh ah-cheh-to.)

Esto no es vino, es vinagre.
(Estoh noh éss beenoh, éss beenágrre.)

J'ai demandé du vin, pas un consommé de bouchons!
(Shay d'manday di van, pazan consommay der boo-shon!)

Ho chiesto del vino non una spremuta di sughero.
(Oh kee-eh-sto dehl veenoh non oona spreh-moo-ta dee soogheh-ro.)

He pedido vino, no un puré de corcho.
(Eh peddeedoh beenoh, noh oon pooré deh córtchoh.)

Dites-donc, c'est des œufs de plésiosaure qu'il y a dans cette omelette?
(Deet-donk, say day zehr der plaizeeozawr keelyar dan set omelette?)

Questa frittata è stata fatta con uova di dinosauro?
(Kweh-sta freet-tah-tah eh stahta fattah cohn oo-oh-va dee dee-noh-za-oo-ro?)

¿Ha hecho esta tortilla con huevos de pterodáctilo?
(Ah étchoh éstah torteellya cón wébos deh pterodácteeloh?)

Donnez-moi donc une cu-vette pour y mettre les vers!
(Donnay mwar donk in kivett poor ee mettr'er lay vair!)

Mi darebbe un piatto a parte per i vermi?
(Mee darehb-beh oon pee-aht-to ah parteh per ee vehr-mee?)

¿Tiene otro plato para dejar los gusanos?
(Teeyéne ótroh plátoh párah dehhár lós goosános?)

C'est l'habitude, dans votre vestiaire, de vendre les meilleurs manteaux?
(Say labeetid, dan vawtr'er vaisteeair, der vandr'er lay maiyehr mantaw?)

Al guardaroba, i cappotti belli vengono venduti tutti?
(Al gooar-dah-roh-ba, ee cahp-pottee behl-lee vehn-gohno vehn-doo-tee toot-tee?)

¿Se vende usted los abri-gos del guardarropa?
(Sé béndeh oostéh lóss abree-gos dél gwardarrópah?)

Vous ne savez pas lire? Elle est à moi cette place!
(Voon savay par leer? Ell ay tar mwar set plass!)

Non sa leggere il numero sul biglietto? Questo è il mio posto.
(Non sah leh-jeh-reh eel noomeh-ro sool bee-lliet-to? Kwehsto eh eel meeoh poh-stoh.)

Si supiera leer la entrada, vería que este asiento es mío.
(See sooppeeyera lé-ér lah entrádah, bereeya ké éste aseeyéntoh éss meeoh.)

AT THE THEATER

Clumsy fool, that's my foot you stepped on.	Sie Tölpel! Das war mein Fuss. *(Zee toelpel! daass vaar myn fuss.)*
Please remove that monstrosity from your head.	Nehmen Sie bitte das monströse Ding von Ihrem Kopf. *(Naymen zee bitte daass monstroeze deenk fon eerem kopf.)*
Blow your dirty smoke somewhere else.	Blasen Sie Ihren grässlichen Zigarettenrauch in eine andere Richtung. *(Blaasen . zee eeren graysslishen tsigaretten-raoch in yne aandere rishtoong.)*
Keep your sticky hands to yourself.	Nehmen Sie Ihre klebrigen Hände weg. *(Naymen zee eere klaybrigen haynde vayk.)*
Stop yapping so that I can hear the play.	Seien Sie endlich still, ich will das Theaterstück hören. *(Zyen zee endlish shtill, ish vill daass teatershtuek hoeren.)*
Keep your candy wrappers to yourself.	Ihr Bonbon-Papier behalten Sie ruhig selbst. *(Eer bong-bong-papeer behaalten-zee roohig saylbst.)*
Boo!	Boo! *(Boo!)*

FRENCH	ITALIAN	SPANISH
Imbécile! C'est mon pied, c'est pas un paillasson! *(Ambaiseel! Say mon peeay, say pazan pahyasson!)*	Disgraziato, questo è il mio piede. *(Dee-sgra-tzeeahto, kwehsto eh eel meeoh pee-eh-deh.)*	¡Idiota! ¿No ve que me está pisando?) *(Eediotah! Noh bé ké mé stá péesándoh?)*
Enlevez-moi donc cette horreur que vous avez sur la tête! *(Anlvay-mwar donk set orehr ker voo zavay sir lar tait!)*	La prego di togliersi quell'orrore che ha in testa. *(Lah pregoh dee toh-lliersee kwel ohr-roh-reh keh ah een teh-sta.)*	¿Quiere quitarse este esperpento de la cabeza? *(Kyére keetarseh ésteh sperpéntoh dé lá kabétha?)*
Allez souffler votre fumée dans le nez de quelqu'un d'autre! *(Allay sooflay vawtr fimmay dan l'nay der kelkan dawtr.)*	Soffi il fumo della sua puzzolente sigaretta da un'altra parte. *(Sohf-fee eel foomo dehl-la soo-ah pootzolehn-teh seegaretta da oon ahltrah parteh.)*	¡Vaya a fumar a otra parte, cochino! *(Báyah ah foomár ah ótrah párteh, cotcheenoh!)*
Promenez vos sales mains ailleurs! *(Promnay vo sal man ahyehr!)*	Si tenga le sue sporche mani in tasca. *(See tehnga leh soo-eh sporkeh mah-nee een tah-ska.)*	¡Métase las manos en los bolsillos! *(Métasse lass mános én loss bolseellyos!)*
Vous avez fini d'aboyer? Je veux l'entendre, moi, cette pièce. *(Voo zavay feenee dabwahyay? Sher vehr lantandr'er, mwar, set peeays.)*	Vuol finirla con le sue chiacchiere e lasciarmi sentire la commedia? *(Voo-ohl fee-neerla con leh soo-eh kiak-kee-eh-reh eh lah-sharmee sehnteereh la cohm-meh-deeah?)*	¡Deje de ladrar, a ver si puedo oir el diálogo! *(Déhhe dé ladrár, ah bér see pwéddo o-eer él deeálogo!)*
Gardez vos épluchures pour vous-même, je ne suis pas votre poubelle! *(Garday vo zaiplishir poor voo-maim, shern swee par vawtr'er poobell!)*	La carta delle sue caramelle se la tenga per sé. *(Lah cartah dehl-leh soo-eh carameh-leh seh lah tehnga per seh.)*	¡Cómase los papeles de los caramelos! *(Kómase loss pahpéles dé loss karamélos!)*
Hou! Hou! *(Oo! Oo!)*	*(In Italy to show disapproval at the theatre one whistles)*	¡Bu! *(Boo!)*

AT THE THEATER

Is this supposed to be an amateur performance?

Das ist wohl eine Amateur-Vorstellung?
(Daass ist vol yne ama-toer-forshtellong?)

Rotten!

Schrecklich.
(Shrayklish.)

This place is a flea bag.

Dieses Theater ist eine Flohkiste.
(Deezes teater ist yne flo-keeste.)

This seat is filthy.

Dieser Sitz ist dreckig.
(Deezer zits ist draykig.)

That's not applause—it's the insects flapping their wings.

Da klatscht keiner Beifall—das ist das Ungeziefer, das mit den Flügeln schlägt.
(Daa klaatsht kyner byfaall—daass eest daass oon-ge-tseefer, daass mit dayn fluegeln shlaygt.)

Keep that dirty coat on your own knees.

Den dreckigen Mantel legen Sie bitte auf Ihre eigenen Kniee.
(Dayn draykigen maantel laygen zee bitte aof eere ygenen cnee-e.)

Move your fat behind.

Bewegen Sie 'mal Ihren dicken Hintern.
(Bewaygen zee maal eeren dicken hintern.)

FRENCH	ITALIAN	SPANISH
C'est des amateurs? *(Say day zammatehr?)*	Sarebbe uno spettacolo di dilettanti questo? *(Sarehb-beh oonoh spehttah-coh-loh dee deelet-tantee kweh-stoh?)*	¡Parece un teatro de aficionados! *(Paréthe oon teátroh dé afeethionádos!)*
Quel four! *(Kel foor!)*	Fa schifo. *(Fa skeefoh.)*	¡Putrefacto! *(Pootrefáctoh!)*
Ce fauteuil est déguelasse! *(Sehr fawtay ay daigehrlass!)*	Questo sedile è lurido. *(Kweh-stoh seh-dee-leh eh loo-ree-doh.)*	Esta butaca está asquerosa. *(Estah bootákah stá askehrósa.)*
Quel trou à puces! *(Kel troo ar pis!)*	Questa sala è infima. *(Kweh-sta sahla eh eenfeema.)*	Este asiento es un nido de pulgas. *(Esteh aseeyéntoh éss oon needoh dé poolgas.)*
Qui c'est qui applaudit? Personne, ce sont les sièges qui craquent. *(Kee say kee applodee? Pairson, sehr son lay seeaysh kee krak.)*	Non è un applauso, sono gli insetti che sbattono le ali. *(Non eh oon ap-plah-oozo, sohno llee een-set-tee keh sbat-tohno leh ah-lee.)*	No son aplausos, son los insectos que baten las alas. *(Noh són applausos, són loss insektos ké báten lass álas.)*
Ça ne vous ferait rien de garder vos sales frusques sur vos genoux! *(Sarn voo fray ryend garday vo sal frisk sir vo shnoo?)*	Si tenga quello sporco cappotto sulle sue ginocchia. *(See tengah kwelloh sporcoh cap-pot-toh soolleh soo-eh jeenock-kia.)*	Ponga este pringoso abrigo en sus rodillas. *(Póngah ésteh preengósoh abreegoh én soos roddeellyas.)*
Allez, bougez-moi donc votre derrière de là! *(Allay, booshay-mwar donk vawtr daireeair der lar!)*	Muova quel deretano. *(Moo-oh-vah kwel deh-rehtah-noh.)*	¡Apártese un poco, queso de bola! *(Apárteseh oon pókoh, késoh dé bólah!)*

79

IN THE BAR

Is all your beer flat?

Haben Sie nur abgestandenes Bier?

(Haabn zee noor abge-shtaandenes beer?)

I asked for a drink, not mouthwash.

Ich wollte etwas zu trinken haben, aber kein Gesöff.

(Ish volte etvaas tsoo trinkn haabn, aabr kyn gezoeff.)

Is this wine or vinegar?

Ist das Wein oder Essig?

(Ist daass vyn odr ayssig?)

Do you water down *all* your liquor?

Verwässern Sie alle Ihre Getränke?

(Vervayssern zee aalle eere getraynke?)

Is it possible to get a *full* glass of beer?

Geht noch ein Rum in mein Bier? Ja? Na, dann füllen Sie es mit Bier auf.

(Gayt noch yn roomm in myn beer? Yaa? Na, daann fuelln zee ayss mit beer aof.)

FRENCH	ITALIAN	SPANISH
Elle est toute éventée, votre bière.	La vostra birra è sempre così fiacca?	¿Sólo tiene cerveza insípida?
(Ell ay toot ayvantay, vawtr'er beeyair!)	*(Lah vo-stra bee-rrah eh sem-preh cozi fee-acka?)*	*(Sóloh teeyéne therbétha eenseepeedah?)*
Dis-donc, j'ai demandé à boire, pas une douche!	Desidero una bibita, non la risciacquatura dei bicchieri.	Quiero algo de beber, no para hacer gárgaras.
(Dee-donk, shay d'manday ar bwar, pazin doosh!)	*(Deh-see-dehro oona bee-beeta, non lah ree-sha-kkwa-toora day beekk-ye-ree.)*	*(Kyéro álgo dé behbér, noh párah athér gárgaras.)*
C'est du vin aigre, ou du vinaigre?	Questo è vino o aceto?	¿Esto es vino o vinagre?
(Say di van aigr'er, oo di veenaigr?)	*(Kwesto eh vee-no o a-cheh-to?)*	*(Estoh éss beenoh oh beenágreh?)*
Dites-donc, vous dénaturez tous vos alcools, comme ça?	Diluite tutte le bevande alcoòliche?	¿Bautiza usted todos los licores?
(Deet-donk, voo dainahtiray too vo zalkol, kom sar?)	*(Dee-loo-eeteh toot-teh leh beh-vandeh alcohol-eekeh?)*	*(Bauteethah oostéh tóddos loss leecóres?)*
Si ça ne vous fait rien, mettez-moi encore un peu de bière. Je n'ai pas besoin de toute cette mousse pour me faire la barbe. (See note.)	Ci starebbe un rum in questa birra? Si? Allora riempite il bicchiere di birra.	¿Puede echarme ron en la cerveza? ¿Si? ¡Pues acabe de llenarme el vaso con cerveza!
(See sarn voo fay ryen, maitay-mwar ankor an pehr der beeyair. Shnay par berswan der toot set moos poor mer fair lar barb.)	*(Chee sta-reh-bbeh oon rhoom in qwesta bee-rrah? See? Ahllo-ra ree-eh-mpeeteh eel bee-kke-eh-reh dee bee-rràh.)*	*(Pwéde etchármeh rhón én lá therbétha? See? Pwés acábeh dé lyenármeh él básoh cón therbétha!)*

NOTE: In France, the beer would be more likely to be served with the froth filling half the glass. Hence the translation above.

IN THE BAR

Do you use thimbles for shot glasses?

Sie messen wohl mit einem Fingerhut ab?

(Zee mayssen vol mit ynem finger-hoot ab?)

I asked for club soda, not bicarbonate of soda.

Ich wollte Sodawasser haben, kein Natron.

(Ich volte sodavassr haabn, kyn naatron.)

That's not a tip; that's my change.

Das ist nicht Ihr Trinkgeld, das ist mein Wechselgeld.

(Daass ist nicht eer treenkgayld, daass ist myn vaykslgayld.)

When you've sobered up a bit, please bring me a drink.

Wenn Sie wieder etwas nüchtern sind, bringen Sie mir etwas zu trinken.

(Venn zee veedr etvaas nuechtern zind, breengn zee mir etvas tsoo trinkn.)

AT THE SERVICE STATION

Is this a garage or a junkyard?

Ist das hier eine Tankstelle oder ein Schrottgeschäft?

(Ist daass heer yne taank-shtelle oder yn shrott-geshayft?)

Don't your mechanics ever wash?

Waschen sich Ihre Mechaniker nie?

(Vashen zich eere mayschaniker nee?)

FRENCH	ITALIAN	SPANISH
Dites-donc, votre mesure de base, c'est le dé à coudre?	Usate ditali come unità di misura?	¿Usa un dedal para medir las bebidas?
(Deet-donk, vawtr merzir der baz, sayl day ar coodr'er?)	*(Ooza-teh dee-tahlee comeh oo-neetah dee mee-soorah?)*	*(Oosah oon dedál parah mehddir lás behbeedas?)*
J'ai demandé du soda, pas du bicarbonate.	Ho chiesto acqua di seltz, non bicarbonato.	He pedido sifón, no bicarbonato.
(Shay d'manday di soda, par di beekarbonatt.)	*(Oh kee-eh-sto a-qua dee seltz, non bee-car-bonah-to.)*	*(Eh peddedoh seephón, noh beecarbonátoh.)*
Eh là! C'est pas le pourboire ça, c'est ma monnaie!	Quella non è la mancia, è il mio resto.	No es la propina, es mi cambio.
(Eh lar! Say parl poorbwar sar, ma mawnay!)	*(Kwe-llah non eh lah mahn-cha, eh eel mee-o rest-o.)*	*(Noh éss lá propeenah, éss mee cámbeeyo.)*
Quand vous vous sentirez mieux, apportez-moi donc à boire, s'il vous plaît.	Quando avete smaltito la sbornia, potreste portarmi da bere?	Cuando tenga tiempo sirvame de beber.
(Kan voo voo santeeray meeyehr, apportay-mwar donk ar bwar, seel voo play.)	*(Kwah-ndo ah-vehteh smah-lteeto lah sbor-nee-ah potreh-steh portah-rmee dah beh-reh?)*	*(Kwándoh téngah teeyém-poh, seerbameh dé behbér.)*
C'est un garage chez vous, ou est-ce que vous faites surtout de la casse?	Questa è un'autorimessa o un deposito di ferri vecchi?	¿Es un taller o un comercio de chatarra?
(Say tan garahsh shay voo, oo aysker voo fait sirtoo d'lar kas?)	*(Kwesta eh oon a-ooto-ree-meh-ssa o oon deposit-o dee feh-rrhee veh-kkee?)*	*(Ess oon tahllyér oh oon comértheeyo dé chatárrah?)*
Ils se lavent parfois, vos mécaniciens?	I vostri meccanici si lavano mai?	¿Se lavan los mecánicos de vez en cuando?
(Eel ser lahv parfwar, vo maikarneesyan?)	*(Ee voh-stree meh-cah-nee-chee see lah-vah-no my?)*	*(Seh lávan lóss mehcáneecos dé béth én kwándoh?)*

AT THE SERVICE STATION

Let me have some gas that hasn't been watered down.

Geben Sie mir Benzin, aber unverdünnt.

(Gaybn zee mir benzeen, aber unferduennt.)

I asked you to fill it up, not hose down the garage with gasoline.

Sie sollen meinen Tank mit dem Benzin auffüllen, nicht ihre Tankstelle damit spritzen.

(Zee zollen mynen taank mit benzeen aof-fuelln, nich eere tankshtelle daamit shpritsen.)

Get your greasy butt off the driver's seat.

Setzten Sie sich nicht mit Ihrem schmierigen Hosenboden in den Wagen.

(Zetsen zee zich nicht mit eerem shmeerign hosenboden in dayn vaagen.)

Do you have a machine that makes all those dents?

Verbeulen Sie die Autos mit einer Spezialmaschine?

(Verboyln zee dee autos mit yner shpetsiaal-maasheene?)

I asked for a mechanic, not a ballet dancer.

Ich habe nach einem Autoschlosser gefragt, nicht nach einem Solotänzer.

(Ich haabe naach ynem autoshlosser gefraagt, nicht naach ynem zolotayntser.)

FRENCH	ITALIAN	SPANISH
Je voudrais bien un peu d'essence, s'il vous plaît, avec pas trop d'eau, si possible. *(Sher voodray byen an pehr daysans, seel voo play, aveck par tro do, see poseebl.)*	Favorisca della benzina senza aggiunta d'acqua. *(Fah-vo-reeska deh-lla benzee-na sehn-tza ah-djown-ta d'a-qua.)*	Quiero gasolina sin agua. *(Kyéro gasoleenah seen ágwah.)*
Je vous ai demandé de faire le plein, pas d'en profiter pour nettoyer votre garage à mes frais! *(Sher voo zay d'manday der fair ler plan, par dan profeetay poor netwahyay vawtr'er garahsh ar may fray!)*	Le ho chiesto di fare il pieno, non di lavare il garage con la benzina. *(Leh oh kee-eh-sto dee far-eh eel pee-ehno, non dee lah-vah-reh eel garah-ge con lah benzee-na.)*	Le he dicho que llenara el depósito, no que lavara el suelo con gasolina. *(Leh eh deetchoh ke llyé-nárah él dehpóseetoh, noh ké lavárah él swéloh cón gasoleenah.)*
Ça ne vous ferait rien de décoller votre derrière et tout le cambouis qu'il y a dessus de ma banquette? *(Sarn voo fray ryen der daikolay vawtr'er daireeair ay tool kambwee keelyar dersi der mar bankett?)*	Si tolga dal posto di guida col suo sporco sedere. *(See tol-ga dahl post-oh dee goo-eedah col soo-oh spork-o seh-deh-reh.)*	Quite su sucio trasero de mi asiento, ¿quiere? *(Keeteh soo sootheeyo trah-séroh dé mee asseeyéntoh, keeyére?)*
Vous avez une machine à calculer pour faire le compte de toutes ces beugnes? *(Voo zavay in masheen ar kalkilay poor fair ler kont der toot say bern'yer?)*	Avete una calcolatrice per contare tutte quelle ammaccature? *(Ah-vehteh oona cahl-co-lah-tree-cheh pehr con-tah-reh too-tteh kweh-lleh ah-mmah-kah-tooreh?)*	¿Tiene usted una máquina de abollar? *(Teeyéne oostéh oonah má-keenah dé ahbóllyár?)*
J'ai demandé un mécani-cien, pas un danseur de ballet! *(Shay d'manday an mai-karneesyan, pazan dansehr der ballay!)*	Mi serve un meccanico, non un ballerino. *(Mee serveh oon meh-cah-nee-co, non oon bah-lleh-ree-no.)*	He pedido un mecánico, no un bailarín. *(Eh peddedoh oon mehca-neecoh, noh oon báylareen.)*

AT THE SERVICE STATION

At last! Did you sleep well?

Endlich. Haben Sie gut geschlafen?
*(Ayntlich. Haabn zee goot ge-
shlaafn?)*

That's not a repair bill; that's your tax return.

Das ist Ihre Steuererklärung
und nicht die Reparaturrechnung.
*(Daass ist eere shtoyrerklairong
oond nicht dee repaaraatoor-
rayshnong.)*

DRIVING

Let me recommend a good optician.

Hier ist die Adresse eines guten
Augenarztes.
*(Heer ist dee addresse ynes gooten
aognaartstes.)*

Move over, you fool.

Können Sie nicht ausweichen,
Sie Idiot?
*(Koennen zee nicht aosvychen, zee
idioot?)*

Road hog!

Strassen-Schnecke.
(Shtraassen-shnayke.)

When does your learner's permit expire?

Sie haben Ihr 'Anfänger'-Schild
verloren.
*(Zee haabn eer anfayngr-sheeld
ferlooren.)*

FRENCH	ITALIAN	SPANISH
Ah vous voilà enfin! J'espère que vous avez bien dormi. *(Ah voo vwalar anfan! Shaispair ker voo zavay byen dormee.)*	Finalmente! Avete dormito bene? *(Feenahl-mehn-teh! Ah-veh-teh dor-mee-to beh-neh?)*	¡Por fin! ¿Ha dormido usted bien? *(Pór feen! Ah dormeedoh oostéh beeyén?)*
Dites-donc, c'est pas une facture ça! C'est votre feuille d'impôts! *(Deet-donk, say pazin faktir sar! Say vawtr fay dampaw!)*	Quello non è un conto riparazioni, è il prezzo di una macchina nuova. *(Kweh-lo non eh oon con-to reepah-rah-tzee-ohnee, eh eel preh-tzo dee oona mah-kkee-na noo-ohva.)*	Esto no es una factura, es el impuesto sobre la renta. *(Estoh nó éss oonah factoo-rah, éss él eempwéstoh só-breh lá réntah.)*
Voici l'adresse d'un excellent oculiste. *(Vwacee ladress dan bon okilist.)*	Vuole l'indirizzo di un bravo oculista? *(Voo-oleh l'een-dee-reetzo dee oon brah-vo oc-oo-leesta?)*	¿Quiere la dirección de un buen oculista? *(Kyére la deerecthión dé oon ocoolistah?)*
Eh con! Tire-toi de là! *(Eh kon! Teer-twar d'lar!)*	Si muova, pezzo di cretino. *(See moo-ohva, peh-tzo dee cretin-o.)*	¡Quítese de ahí, idiota! *(Keetehseh dé a-ee, eedeeó-tah!)*
Chauffard! *(Shaufahr!)*	Criminale! *(Cree-mee-nah-leh.)*	¡Mamarracho! *(Mamarráchoh!)*
NOTE: No L-plates in France. *However, a possible insult might be:* Vas donc, bleu! *(Var-donk, bler!)*	La patente quando la prende? *(Lah pah-tehn-teh kwahn-do lah prehn-deh?)*	Si no sabe conducir, tire de un carro. *(See nó sábeh condootheer, teereh dé oon cárroh.)*

DRIVING

Do you always drive with your feet?

Fahren Sie immer nur mit den Füssen?

(Faarn zee immer noor mit dayn fuessn?)

AT THE BARBERSHOP/HAIRDRESSER

How many ears have you cut off today?

Wieviele Ohren haben Sie denn heute schon abgeschnitten?

(Veefeele oren haaben zee denn hoyte shon abgeshnitten?)

Do you buy your bandages wholesale?

Kaufen Sie Ihre Verbands-Pflaster im Grosshandel ein?

(Kaofen zee eere ferbaands-pflaster im groshaandl yn?)

Do you always drive with your feet?

FRENCH	ITALIAN	SPANISH

FRENCH

Vous conduisez toujours comme un pied?
(Voo kondweezay tooshoor kom an peeay?)

ITALIAN

Guida sempre con i piedi?
(Goo-eedah sehm-preh con ee pee-ehdee?)

SPANISH

¿Siempre conduce con los pies?
(Seeyémpreh conootheh cón loss peeyés?)

Combien d'oreilles avez-vous coupé aujourd'hui?
(Kombyen doray avay-voo coopay oshoordwee?)

Quante orecchie ha tagliato oggi?
(Kwahn-teh oreh-kee-eh ah tah-liah-to oh-djee?)

¿Cuántas orejas ha cortado hoy?
(Kwántas oréhhas ah cortádoh óy?)

Vous l'achetez au mètre, le sparadrap?
(Voo lashtay o maitr, ler sparadra?)

Il cerotto lo comprate all'ingrosso, qui?
(Eel tcheh-roh-to lo comprah-teh ahll'een-gro-sso, kwee?)

¿Compra usted el fijapelo en los encantes?
(Cómprah oostéh él feehhapéloh én loss encántes?)

AT THE BARBERSHOP/HAIRDRESSER

Is this a hair dryer or an oven?

Ist das ein Haartrockner oder ein Backofen?

(Ist daass yn haar-troc-ner oder yn baackofen?)

Don't you ever wash your combs and brushes?

Waschen Sie Ihre Kämme und Bürsten nie?

(Vashen zee eere kaymme oond buerstn nee?)

I wanted to be shaved, not scraped.

Rasieren sollten Sie mich, nicht schmirgeln.

(Raazeeren zolten zee mish, nisht shmeergeln.)

I asked for a manicure, not an amputation

Maniküren sollen Sie, nicht amputieren.

(Maaneekuern zollen zee, nisht aampooteeren.)

That towel is filthy.

Das Handtuch ist dreckig.

(Daass haandtooch ist draykig.)

Have you ever cut anyone's hair before?

Haben Sie schon einmal Haare geschnitten?

(Haabn zee shon ynmaal haare ge-shnittn?)

Do you catch fish in this hair net?

Fangen Sie mit dem Haarnetz auch Fische?

(Faangn zee mit daym haarnets aoch fishe?)

FRENCH	ITALIAN	SPANISH
C'est un séchoir ou un four? *(Say tan saishwar oo an foor?)*	Questo è un casco o un forno? *(Kwesto eh oon cask-o o oon for-noh?)*	¿Esto es un secador o un hornillo? *(Estoh éss oon sehkadór oh oon orneellyo?)*
Vous les trempez parfois dans de l'eau savonneuse, vos peignes et brosses? *(Voo lay trampay parfwar dand law savonerz, vo pain ay bros?)*	I pettini e le spazzole non li lavate proprio mai? *(Ee peh-tee-nee eh leh spah-tzo-leh non lee lah-vahteh pro-pree-oh my?)*	¿No lava nunca los peines ni los cepillos? *(Noh lávah nooncah lóss péyness nee lóss thepeellyos?)*
Dites-donc, vous me rasez ou vous me raclez? *(Deet-donk, voom rahzay oo voo mer raklay?)*	Le ho chiesto di farmi la barba, non di piallarmi. *(Leh ho kee-ehsto dee fahr-mee lah bar-bah, non dee pee-allah-rmee.)*	Quiero que me afeite, no que me deshuelle. *(Kyéroh ké mé aphéyteh, noh ké mé deswéllye.)*
J'ai demandé un manucure, pas une amputation. *(Shay d'manday an mani-kir, pazin ampitasyon.)*	Le ho chiesto di farmi le mani, non di amputarmele. *(Leh oh kee-ehsto dee fahr-mee leh mah-nee, non dee ah-mpoo-tar-meh-leh.)*	Quiero que me haga la manicura, no una ampu-tación. *(Kyéroh ké mé ágah lá manykoorah, nó oonah am-pootathión.)*
Cette serviette est cradot! *(Set serviette ay krado!)*	Quell'asciugamano fa schifo. *(Kwel ah-shoo-gahmah-no fah skee-fo.)*	Esta toalla está sucia. *(Estah toahllya stá soo-thiah.)*
Je parie que c'est la premiè-re fois que vous le faites! *(Shparee ker say lar prermy-air fwar ker vool fait!)*	È la prima volta che taglia i capelli? *(Eh lah pree-ma vol-ta keh tah-liah ee cah-peh-lee?)*	¿Ha cortado alguna vez el pelo? *(Ah cortádoh algoonah béth él péloh?)*
Vous vous en servez pour la pêche, ce filet? *(Voo voo zan sairvay poor lar paish, ser feelay?)*	Con questa rete riesce a prender pesci? *(Con kwesta reh-teh ree-ehsheh ah prehn-dehr peh-shee?)*	¿Va a pescar con esta rede-cilla? *(Bá ah pescár cón éstah rehdethillya?)*

AT THE BARBERSHOP/HAIRDRESSER

Hurry up—I came here for a haircut not a siesta.

Beeilen Sie sich! Ich bin zum Haarschneiden hergekommen, nicht zum Ausruhen.

(Be-ylen zee zeesh! ish bin tsoom haar-shnydn hairgekommen, neesht tsoom aosroo-n.)

I'd rather have my own coat, if you don't mind.

Ich möchte meinen eigenen Mantel haben, wenn's Ihnen nichts ausmacht.

(Ish moe-shte mynen ygenen maantl haaben, vaynn's eenen nishts aosmaacht.)

These are the straightest curls I've ever seen.

Das sind die glattesten Locken, die ich je gesehen habe.

(Daass zind dee glaattesten lockn, dee ish yeah ge-zayn haabe.)

Do I get my money back if I go bald?

Bekomme ich mein Geld wieder, wenn ich alle Haare verliere?

(Bekomme ish myn gayld veeder, venn ish aalle haare ferleere?)

Where do you place bets on the flea races in this joint?

Wo kann man hier eine Wette für Ihre Flohrennen placieren?

(Vo kaann maann heer yne vette fuer eere flo-raynnen plaasseeren?)

Were you a professional wrestler before you became a hairdresser?

Waren Sie Freistil-Ringkämpfer, ehe Sie Friseur wurden?

(Vaaren zee fryshteel-ring-kaympffer, ay-he zee freesoer voordn?)

FRENCH	ITALIAN	SPANISH
Allez! Magnez-vous un peu! Je ne suis pas venu pour la sieste!	Si spicci, sono venuta a farmi pettinare, non a far la siesta.	¡Dése prisa! ¡He venido a cortarme el pelo, no a dormir la siesta!
(Allay! Maneeay-voo an per! Shern swee par verni poor lar seeaist!)	*(See speechee, sono veh-noo-ta ah far-mee peh-tee-nah-reh, non ah far lah siesta.)*	*(Déseh preesah! Eh beneedoh a cortármeh él péloh, nó ah dormeer lá seeyéstah.)*
Je préférerais mon manteau, vous savez!	Se non le dispiace, vorrei il *mio* cappotto.	Quiero mi abrigo, si no le importa.
(Sher praifair'ray mon mantaw, voo savay!)	*(Seh non leh dees-pee-ah-cheh, vo-rray eel mee-o cah-pot-toh.)*	*(Kyéroh mee abreegoh, see nó lé eempórtah.)*
Ce sont les boucles les plus raides que j'ai jamais vues!	Questi sono i ricci più diritti che ho mai visto.	Son los rizos más tiesos que jamás he visto.
(Ser son lay bookl'er lay pli raid ker shay sharmay vi!)	*(Kwesto sono ee rec-tchee pew dee-ree-tee keh oh my vee-sto.)*	*(Són lóss reethos máss tesyésos ké hamáss eh beestoh.)*
Vous me remboursez si je deviens chauve?	Se dopo divento calva, mi restituisce il denaro?	¿Me devolverá el dinero si me quedo calvo?
(Voom ramboorsay seesh dervyen shauv?)	*(Seh dopo dee-ven-to cahl-va, mee reh-stee-too-ee-sheh eel deh-nah-ro?)*	*(Mé debolbehrá él deenéroh seé mé kédoh cálboh?)*
Vous avez un P.M.U. pour vos puces?	Si fanno scommesse sulle pulci in questo locale?	¿Se admiten apuestas para las carreras de pulgas en este establecimiento?
(Voo zavay an PAY.EM.I. poor vo pis?)	*(See fah-nno scoh-meh-sseh soo-leh pool-chee in kwesto local-eh?)*	*(Sé atmeeten apwéstas párah láss carréras dé poolgass én ésteh stabblethimeeyéntoh?)*
Vous faisiez du catch avant de vous faire coiffeur?	Prima di diventare parrucchiere faceva la lotta libera?	¿Era usted luchador de lucha libre antes de ser peluquero?
(Voo fehsyay di catch avand voo fair kwafehr?)	*(Pree-mah dee dee-ven-tah-reh pah-rroo-kiereh fah-cheh-va lah loh-ttah lee-beh-ra?)*	*(Erah oostéh lootchahdor de lootchah leebreh ántess dé sér pehlookéroh?)*

93

AT THE BANK/POST OFFICE

Don't you know how to count, you fool?

Können Sie nicht zählen, Sie Dummer?
(Koennen zee nisht tsaylen, zee doommer?)

I'd like some clean money while you're at it.

Wo Sie gerade dabei sind: geben Sie mir, bitte, saubere Scheine.
(Vo zee ge-raade daaby zeend: gayben zee meer, bitte zaobre shyne.)

Did you enjoy your nap?

Haben Sie gut geschlafen?
(Haaben zee goot ge-shlaafen?)

The rest of my change would be nice now, please.

Und nun hätte ich gern den Rest des Wechselgeldes, bitteschön.
(Oond noon haytte ish gairn dayn rest days vaykselgayldes, bitte-shoen.)

Do you short-change everybody here?

Geben Sie hier jedem zu knapp raus?
(Gayben zee heer yaydem tsoo cnaapp raos?)

I'll lick my own stamps.

Meine Marken lecke ich selber.
(Myne maarken laycke ish saylber.)

94

FRENCH	ITALIAN	SPANISH
Dites-donc, vous savez compter? *(Deet-donk, voo savay kontay?)*	Non sa contare, stupido. *(Non sah con-tah-reh, stoópeedo.)*	¿Es que no sabe contar, imbécil? *(Ess ké nó sábeh contár, imbéthill?)*
Je ne refuserai pas des billets neufs, vous savez! *(Shern refizray par day beeyeh nerf, voo savay!)*	Se non le chiedo troppo, vorrei delle banconote pulite. *(Seh non leh kie-doh troppo, voh-rray deh-lleh bah-nkono-teh poo-lee-teh.)*	Quisiera billetes limpios antes de que los ensucie todos. *(Keeseeyéra billyétes límpeeyos ántes dé ké loss ensoothieh tóddos.)*
Alors? On a bien dormi? *(Alohr? On ar byen dormee?)*	Ha fatto un bel pisolino? *(Ah fah-tto oon behl pee-so-lee-no?)*	¿Ha dormido bien hasta ahora? *(Ah dormeedoh beeyén ástah aórah?)*
Je ne dirai pas non, si vous me rendiez la monnaie. *(Shern deeray par non, see voom randyay lar mawnay.)*	E ora, se finisse di darmi il resto non lo rifiuterei. *(Eh ora, seh fee-nee-sseh dee dahr-mee eel resto-o, non lo ree-few-teh-ray.)*	Le agradecería que me devolviera todo el cambio. *(Leh agrahdethería ké médebohlbeeyérah tóddo él kambeeyo.)*
Dites-moi, vous rognez un peu la monnaie de tout le monde ici, non? *(Deet-mwar, voo ronyay an pehr lar mawnay der tool mond eecee, non?)*	Sbagliate nel dare il resto a tutti qui? *(Sbah-lia-teh nehl dah-reh eel rest-o ah too-ttee kwi?)*	¿Siempre devuelven menos de lo debido? *(Seeyémpreh debwélben ménos dé ló dehbeedoh?)*
Je lécherai mes timbres moi-même. *(Sher laishray may tambr'er mwar-maim.)*	I francobolli me li lecco da me. *(Ee frah-nco-bollee meh lee leh-ko dah meh.)*	Mis sellos quiero lamerlos yo solo. *(Mees sellyos kyéroh lamérloss yó sóloh.)*

IN THE PUBLIC RESTROOM

This place is filthy.

Verdreckt ist es hier.
(Ferdrayckt ist es heer.)

This place stinks.

Hier stinkt es.
(Heer shtingt ays.)

Don't you have clean sinks?

Gibt's hier keine sauberen Waschbecken?
(Geebt's heer kyne zaobren vashbaycken?)

How about a clean towel?

Und wo ist ein sauberes Handtuch?
(Oond vo ist yn zaobres haandtooch?)

Do you use a real soap here or just this gook?

Haben Sie hier auch richtige Seife oder nur diesen Mist?
(Haabn zee heer aoch reeshtige zyfe oder noor deesen meesst?)

Do you write all those dirty poems on the wall yourself?

Schreiben Sie diese anstössigen Gedichte alle an die Wand?
(Shryben zee deeze aanshtoesseegen gedichte aalle an dee vaand?)

Keep away, you dirty pervert.

Halten Sie mir diesen widerlichen Schwulen vom Leib.
(Haalten zee meer deesen veederlishn shvoolen fom lyb.)

Don't you ever clean this place?

Machen Sie hier nie sauber?
Maachen zee heer nee zaober?)

FRENCH	ITALIAN	SPANISH

Pouah! C'est dégueulasse!
(Pwah! Say daigehrlahss!)

Questo gabinetto è schifoso.
(Kwesto gah-bee-neh-to eh skee-foso.)

Esto está hecho un asco.
(Estoh stá étchoh oon áscoh.)

Ça pue!
(Sar pi!)

Questo gabinetto puzza.
(Kwesto gah-bee-neh-to poo-tza.)

Aquí huele a mierda.
(Akee wélleh ah meeyérdah.)

Vous n'avez aucun lavabo propre?
(Voo navay okan lahvahbo prawpr?)

I lavandini puliti non esistono?
(Ee lava-ndee-nee poo-lee-tee non eh-sees-tono?)

¿No hay ningún urinario limpio?
(Nó áy neengoon urinár-reeyo límpeeyo?)

Et si je vous demandais une serviette propre?
Eh seesh sher voo d'manday in serviette prawpr?)

Che ne direbbe di un asciugamano pulito?
(Keh neh dee-re-bbe dee oon a-shoe-gah-mahno poo-leeto?)

¿Tiene toallas limpias?
(Teeyénne toállyas límpee-yas?)

Vous avez du vrai savon ou on se contente de ce bout de lard visqueux?
(Voo zavay di vray sarvon oo on sehr contant der sehr bood lar veeskehr?)

Si può avere del sapone o c'è solo questa porcheria?
(See pwò ah-vehreh dehl sah-po-neh oh cheh solo qwesta pork-eh-rya?)

¿Tienen jabón o sólo usan estiércol?
(Teeyénn habón oh sóloh oosan esteeyércol?)

C'est vous le poète des chiottes?
(Say vool po'ett day sheott?)

È lei il poeta che scrive quei versi osceni sul muro?
(Eh lay eel poh-eh-ta keh scree-veh kwe-ee vers-ee oh-sheh-nee soo-ee moo-ree?)

¿Escribe usted mismo estos versos en la pared?
(Screebeh oostéh meesmoh éstos bérsos én lá pahrët?)

Vas te faire voir ailleurs, foutue pédale!
(Vat fair vwar ayehr, footi paidal!)

Mi stia alla larga, sporco pervertito.
(Me stee-a allah lah-rgah, spork-o per-vehr-tee-to.)

Puede quedarse con su podredumbre.
(Pwédeh kedárseh cón soo podrehdoombreh.)

Vous nettoyez souvent, à ce que je vois!
(Voo netwahyay soovan, ar skersh vwar!)

Non fate mai pulizia qui?
(Non fah-teh my poo-lee-tzee-ah kwi?)

¿Nunca limpian este lugar?
(Noonkah límpeeyan ésteh loogár?)

AT THE OFFICE

Did you type this with your feet?

Haben Sie das mit den Füssen getippt?
(Haaben zee daass mit dayn fuessen getippt?)

I asked for a letter, not a set of fingerprints.

Ich will einen Brief sehen, nicht Ihre dreckigen Fingerabdrücke.
(Ish vil ynen breef sayhen, nisht eere draykigen fingeraabdruecke.)

Stop listening in on the phone.

Geh'n Sie aus meiner Leitung raus.
(Gayn zee aos myner lytong raos.)

Don't you ever try to earn your salary?

Haben Sie schon 'mal versucht, Ihr Geld wirklich zu verdienen?
(Haaben zee shon maal ferzoocht, eer gayld virklish tsoo ferdeenen?)

Do you always sleep at the office?

Schlafen Sie immer im Büro?
(Shlaafen zee immer im buro?)

You're not qualified to shovel manure.

Sie sind ja nicht einmal zum Mistkarren brauchbar.
(Zee sind yaa nisht maal tsoom mistkaarrn braochbaar.)

Late again, you miserable snail!

Wieder spät, Sie müde Schnecke.
(Veeder shpayt, zee muede shnaycke.)

FRENCH	ITALIAN	SPANISH

Elle est à pédale, votre machine à écrire?
(Ell ay tar paidal, vawtr masheen ah aikreer?)

L'ha dattiloscritta coi piedi?
(L'ah dah-ttee-lo-scree-ta co-ee pee-eh-dee?)

¿Ha escrito esto con los pies?
(Ah screetoh éstoh cón loss peeyés?)

Je veux une vraie lettre, pas un brouillon crasseux de vos empreintes digitales.
(Sher vehr zin vray letr, pazan brooyon krahsehr der vo zamprant deesheetal.)

Volevo una lettera, non le sue impronte digitali.
(Vo-leh-vo oona letteh-ra, non leh soo-eh imp-ron-teh dee-gee-tahlee.)

Le he pedido una carta, no sus huellas digitales.
(Lé eh peddeedoh oona cártah, nó soos wéllyas digitáles.)

Vous, avez fini de jouer les concierges sur ma ligne?
(Voo zavay feenee der shoo-ay lay konsyairsh sir mar leen?)

Smetta di ascoltare la mia telefonata all'altro apparecchio.
(Smeh-tta dee ah-scol-tah-reh lah mee-a telephon-ah-tah ahll'ahl-tro ah-ppah-reh-kio.)

Deje de escuchar por el supletorio.
(Déhheh dé scootchár pór él sooplehtóryoh.)

Vous n'avez jamais essayé de *gagner* votre salaire?
(Voo navay shahmay essayay der ganyay vawtr salair?)

Il suo stipendio non cerca mai di guadagnarselo?
(Eel soo-oh stee-pend-yo non cheh-rka my dee gwa-dah-nya-rseh-lo?)

¿No ha intentado nunca ganarse el sueldo?
(Noh ah intentádoh noonkah gahnárseh él swéldoh?)

Vous dormez souvent au bureau?
(Voo dormay soovan o biraw?)

In ufficio, lei dorme sempre?
(In oo-fee-cho, lay dormeh seh-mpreh?)

¿Siempre duerme en la oficina?
(Seeyémpre dwérmeh én lá offeetheenah?)

Vous n'êtes même pas bon pour décharger du fumier.
(Voo nait maim par bon poór daisharshay di fimyay.)

Lei non potrebbe neanche fare lo spazzino.
(Lay non po-treh-bbeh neh-ah-nkeh far-eh lo spa-tzee-no.)

¡Más le valdría sacudir toda esta porquería!
(Máss lé baldreeya sakoodeer tóddah éstah porkehreeya!)

Encore en retard, flemmard!
(Ankor an r'tahr, flemmahr!)

Ecco la tartaruga, di nuovo in ritardo.
(Ekko lah tart-ah-roo-gah, dee noo-ovo in ree-tardo.)

¡Otra vez tarde, miserable tortuga!
(Ótrah béth tárdeh, miserábble tortoogah!)

AT THE OFFICE

Go learn some manners.

Machen Sie, dass Sie rauskommen, und lernen Sie Manieren.

(Maachen zee, daass zee raoskommen, oond lairnen zee maaneern.)

Stop scratching your ass.

Hören Sie endlich auf, Ihr Hinterteil zu kratzen.

(Hoern zee endlish aof, eer hintertyl tsoo kraatsen.)

SPORTS EVENTS

Kill the referee!

Knallt diesen üblen Schiedsrichter ab.

(Chaallt deesen ueblen shcedsrichter aap.)

How much did the other team pay you to lose?

Was zahlt Ihnen die Gegenmannschaft für's Liegenbleiben?

(Vas tsaalt eenen dee gaygnmaannshaft fuer's leegnblybn?)

Foul!

Faul!

(Foul!)

You play dirtier than anyone I've ever seen.

Ihr seid die niederträchtigsten Spieler, die ich je sah.

(Eer zyd dee needrtrayshtigstn shpeeler, dee ish yeah zaa.)

FRENCH	ITALIAN	SPANISH
Sortez! Et allez apprendre la politesse. *(Sortay! Ay allay apprandr lar poleetaiss!)*	Vada a imparare un po' d'educazione. *(Vah-da ah imp-ah-rah-reh oon poh d'e-doo-cah-tzee-oneh.)*	¡Vaya a que le enseñen buenos modales! *(Báyah ah ké lé ensényen bwénos moddáles!)*
T'as fini de te gratter le cul? *(Tar feenee dert gratay lehr ki?)*	Smetta di grattarsi il sedere. *(Smeh-tah dee grah-tahr-see eel seh-dehreh.)*	¡Déje ya de rascarse el culo! *(Déhheh yá dé rascárseh él kooloh!)*
L'arbitre, au poteau! *(Larbeetr, o potaw!)*	Ammazza l'arbitro! *(Ah-mma-tzah l'àh-rbee-tro!)*	¡Cárguense a este maldito árbitro! *(Cárrguenseh ah ésteh mal deetoh árbeetroh!)*
On vous a donné combien pour perdre? *(On voo zar donnay kom-byen poor pairdr?)*	Quanto ti ha pagato l'altra squadra per far finta di star male? *(Kwah-nto tee ah pah-gah-to l'ah-ltrah squah-drah per far feentah dee stahr mah-leh?)*	¿Cuánto te han pagado los del otro equipo? *(Kwántoh té ahn pagádoh loss dél ótroh ekeepoh?)*
No single equivalent. Spectators shout Coup franc! *(free kick)*; Penalty! Corner! *etc.* *(Koo fran! Penaltee! Cornair!)*	Fallo! *(Fah-llo!)*	¡Cochino! *(Cotcheenoh!)*
Vous êtes le joueur le plus salaud que j'aie jamais vu! *(Voo zait ler shooehr ler pli sahlaw ker shay sharmay vi!)*	Sei il giocatore piú sporco che conosca! *(Say eel joh-cah-to-reh pew spork-o keh cono-scah!)*	Eres el jugador más marrano que he visto. *(Érehs él hooghadór máss mahrránoh ké eh beestoh.)*

SPORTS EVENTS

Is this a football (soccer) game or a flea circus?

Ist das Fussballspiel oder ein Flohzirkus?

(Ist daass yn foosbaall-shpeel oder yn flotsirkoos?)

That's right—hit him when the referee isn't looking.

Richtig, hau' ihm eine, wenn der Schiedsrichter nicht guckt.

(Reeshtig, hao eem yne, venn dair sheedsrishter nisht gookt.)

Is this your first-string team or a bunch of rookies?

Ist das Ihre erste oder eine Knabenmannschaft?

(Ist daass eere erste oder yne cnaabn-maannshaft?)

If you can't pay up, you'd better start running.

Für welche Seite laufen Sie denn eigentlich.

(Fuer velshe syte laofn zee denn ygentlish?)

Hit him on the head; he'll never notice.

Knall' ihm eine, der merkt's ja doch nicht.

(Cnaall eem yne, dair mairkts yaa doch nisht.)

THE BEACH

This ice cream tastes like soap.

Dieses Eis schmeckt nach Seife.
(Deeses ice shmaykt nach zyfe.)

FRENCH	ITALIAN	SPANISH
C'est un match de football, ou un cirque? *(Saitan match der football, oo an seerk?)*	Ma questa è una partita di calcio o uno spettacolo di pulci addomesticate? *(Mah questa eh oona pahr-tee-ta dee cah-lchoh o oo-no spéh-ttah-colo dee pool-chee ah-do-meh-stee-cahteh?)*	¿Es un partido de fútbol o un concurso de pulgas? *(Ess oon parteedoh dé football ó oon conkoorsoh deh poolgass?)*
Salaud! C'est ça! Tu lui tombes dessus quand l'arbitre ne voit pas! *(Sahlaw! Say sar! Ti lwee tomb dersi kan larbeetr ner vwar par!)*	Bravo, colpiscilo quando l'arbitro non guarda! *(Bravo, col-pée-she-lo kwahn-do l'ah-rbee-tro non gwah-rdah!)*	¡Pégale, ahora que el árbitro no lo ve! *(Péggaleh, aórah ké él árbeetroh nó ló béh!)*
C'est ça votre meilleure équipe? Ou c'est un ramassis de juniors? *(Say sar vawtr'er maiyehr aikeep? Oo saitan ramasee der shinyawr?)*	Questa è la vostra squadra migliore o sono ragazzi di scuola? *(Kwesta eh lah vo-strah squah-drah millio-reh o sono rah-gah-tzee dee skwo-lah?)*	¿Es la primera vez que juegan los once? *(Ess lah preemérah béth ké whégan loss óntheh?)*
No equivalent, but say: Crache d'abord et fous le camp ensuite! *(Pay up and go!)* *(Crash dabor ay foo ler com onsweet!)*	Sei bravo a scappare! *(Say bravo ah scapa-reh!)*	Por lo visto ha sido corredor de zapatos. *(Pór ló beestoh ah seedoh correhdór dé thapátoss.)*
Tu peux l'assommer, il ne s'en rendra pas compte! *(Ti pehr lasommay, eel ner san randrar par kont!)*	Dagli un colpo in testa, tanto non se ne accorge! *(Dah-llee oon col-poh in teh-stah, tahn-to non seh neh ack-oh-rjeh!)*	¡Rómpele la crisma, no se dará cuenta! *(Rrómpehleh lá creesmah, nó sé dahrá kwéntah!)*
On dirait du savon, cette glace! *(On deeray di savon, set glahs!)*	Questo gelato sa di sapone. *(Questo je-lah-to sah´ dee sah-po-neh.)*	Este helado sabe a jabón. (Estay ayládtho sábeh a habbón.)

THE BEACH

Move your fat carcass so I can get some sun.

Rutschen Sie mal weiter mit Ihrem fetten Kadaver, Sie nehmen mir die Sonne weg.

(Rootshn zee maal vyter mit eerem fayttn cadaver, zee naymen mir dee zonne vayg.)

Did your dog have an accident on these deck chairs?

Auf diesen Liegenstühlen haben sich wohl erst Hunde verewigt?

(Aof deesen leegeshtuelen haabn zish vol airst hoonde ferayvigt?)

Disinfectant might get rid of your smell.

Probieren Sie ' doch 'mal ein Desinfektionsmittel gegen Ihren Körpergeruch.

(Probeeren zee doch maal yn desinfektsions-mittl gaygn eeren koerper-grooch.)

You poor deaf thing, isn't the radio loud enough?

Sie Armer, sind Sie taub? Ist das Radio immer noch nicht laut genug?

(Zee armer, zind zee taob? ist daass raadio immer noch nisht laot genoog?)

The toilet is over there, not in the sea (ocean).

Die Toilette ist da drüben, nicht im Wasser.

(Dee toalette ist daa druebn, nisht im vaasser.)

AT THE PARTY/DANCE

Are you old enough to be out this late, young man?

Dürfen Sie denn überhaupt so spät ausgehen, junger Mann?

(Duerfn zee denn uebrhaopt zo shpayt aosgayn, yoongr maann?)

FRENCH	ITALIAN	SPANISH
Eh, gros! Enlève-toi de mon soleil!	Si muova, grassone, voglio anch'io del sole.	¡Apártese, gordinflón, a ver si me da el sol!
(Eh, gro! Anlaiv-twar d'mon solaiy!)	*(See moo-ovah, grass-oneh, voh-lioh ahn-k-éeoh dehl soleh.)*	*(Apártehseh, gordeenflón, ah bér see mé dá él sól!)*
Merde! Encore un chien qui s'est oublié sur ces chaises-longues!	Su queste sdraio hanno fatto i loro bisogni dei cani?	Parece que se hayan meado los perros en estas gandulas.
(Maird! Ankor an shyen kee set oobleeyay sir say shaiz-long!)	*(Soo kweh-steh sdrah-yoh ah-no fah-to ee loro bee-so-niee day cah-nee?)*	*(Parétheh ké sé áyan meádoh lóss pérros én éstas gandoo-las.)*
Essayez le Crésyl pour vos odeurs!	Faccia il bagno nel di-sinfettante se vuol puzzare meno.	¿Por qué no prueba un desinfectante, a ver si huele mejor?
(Essaiyay ler krezeel poor vo zodehr!)	*(Fah-tchah eel bah-nioh nehl disinfe-ttahn-teh seh voo-ol poo-tzah-reh mehno.)*	*(Pór ké nó prwéba oon desinfectánteh, ah bér see welle mehhór?)*
Eh, sourdingue! Elle hurle pas encore assez ta radio?	Ma lei è sordo? Non la sente quella radio come strepita?	¡Eh, pedazo de tapia! ¿No puede bajar la radio?
(Eh, soordang! Ell irl par zankor assay tar rahdio?)	*(Mah lay eh sordo? Non lah sehn-teh kwe-la rah-dio comeh stréhpeeta?)*	*(Eh, pedáthoh dé táppya! Nó pwédeh bahhár la rá-dioh?)*
Dites-donc vous, les w.c. c'est là-bas, pas dans la mer!	Il gabinetto è da quella parte, non in mare.	El retrete está allí, no en el mar.
(Deet-donk voo, lay vaisay say lah-bar, par dan la mair!)	*(Eel gabinett-o eh dah kweh-lla part-eh, non in mah-reh.)*	*(El retréteh stá allyí, noh én él már.)*
Pas encore couché, jeune homme?	Sei grande abbastanza per star fuori cosí tardi, ra-gazzino?	¿Ya le dejan salir a estas horas, jovencito?
(Pazankor cooshay, shern om?)	*(Say grahn-deh ah-bba-stanza per stah-r fwo-ree cozí tard-ee, rah-gah-tzéeno?)*	*(Yá lé déhhan saleer ah éstas óras, hobentheetoh?)*

AT THE PARTY/DANCE

You have feet like an elephant.

Sie haben ja Elefantenfüsse.
(Zee haabn yaa elephantn-fuesse.)

Keep your wandering paws to yourself.

Hören Sie 'mal mit der Fummelei auf.
(Hoern zee maal meet dair foommely aof.)

You have feet like an elephant.

FRENCH	ITALIAN	SPANISH
Vous avez des pieds d'éléphant. *(Voo zavay day peeyay d' elephan.)*	Ha dei piedi da elefante. *(Ah day pee-eh-dee dah elephánt-eh.)*	Tiene los pies como un elefante. *(Teeyéne lóss peeyés cómoh oon elephánteh.)*
Vous avez fini de me peloter! *(Voo zavay feenee d'mer perlotay?)*	Tenga le mani a posto. *(Teh-ngah leh mah-ny ah posto.)*	Guarde sus pezuñas para otra ocasión. *(Guárdeh soos pehthoonyas párah ótrah ocassión.)*

AT THE PARTY/DANCE

Pour your drink all over someone else.

Müssen Sie Ihr Getränk unbedingt über mich schütten?
(Muessen zee eer getraynk oonbedingt uebr meesh shuettn?)

Do you have a magnifying glass? I'm looking for the buffet.

Ist das das kalte Buffet? Haben Sie ein Vergrösserungsglas?
(Ist daass daass kaalte bueffay? Haabn zee yn fergroesserongsglaass?)

Excellent water you have here.

Vorzügliches Wasser gibt's hier.
(Forssuegleeshes vaasser geebt's heer.)

AT THE BOOKSTORE

Do you tear all your newspapers?

Zerreissen Sie immer erst Ihre Zeitungen?
(Tser-ryssen zee immr airst eere tsytongn?)

Can't you count?

Können Sie nicht rechnen?
(Koennen zee nisht rayshnen?

These must be second-hand.

Das sind natürlich alles gebrauchte Bücher.
(Daass zind naatuerlish aalles gebraochte bueshr.)

FRENCH	ITALIAN	SPANISH
Allez vider votre verre sur quelqu'un d'autre! *(Allay veeday vawtr vair sir kelkan dawtr!)*	La sua bibita le dispiacerebbe versarla su qualcun altro? *(Lah soo-ah bée-bee-ta leh dis-pee-áh-chehre-bbeh versah-rlah soo kwahl-koon ahltro?)*	Vierta la bebida sobre cualquier otro. *(Beeyértah lá behbeedah sóbre kwalkeeyer otroh.)*
Vous avez une loupe? Je cherche le buffet. *(Voo zavay in loop? Sher shairsh ler biffay.)*	È il buffet questo? Scusi, ha una lente d'ingrandimento? *(Eh il boo-ffè qwesto? Scoosee, ah oona lent-eh d'ingrahn-dee-ment-o?)*	¿Esto es el bufete? ¿Dónde está la lupa? *(Estoh éss él booféhteh? Dóndeh stá lá loopah?)*
Y a pas à dire, l'eau est bonne! *(Yah pazah deer, lo ay bonn!)*	Squisita l'acqua che avete qui. *(Squee-see-tah l'aqua keh ah-veh-te kwi.)*	Tienen una agua excelente. *(Teeyénen oonah ágwah ecsehlénteh.)*
Vous avez des journaux qui ne soient pas déchirés? *(Voo zavay day shoorno keen swar par daisheeray?)*	Li strappate apposta i giornali? *(Lee strah-ppah-teh app-ostah ee jor-nah-lee?)*	¿Se dedica a romper todos los periódicos? *(Seh dehdeecah a rompér tóddos loss pereeyódicoss?)*
Vous savez compter? *(Voo savay kontay?)*	Non sa contare? *(Non sah con-tah-reh?)*	¿No sabe contar? *(Noh sábeh contár?)*
Ils sont tous d'occasion, bien sûr? *(Eel son toos dokazyon, byen sir?)*	Presumo che siano tutti di seconda mano. *(Preh-soo-mo keh see-ah-no too-tee dee second-ah mahno.)*	¡Claro! ¡Son de segunda mano! *(Clároh! Són dé segoondah mánoh!)*

AT THE BOOKSTORE

Do you only sell pornography?

Sie verkaufen wohl nur Porno-graphie?

(Zee ferkaofen vol noor porno-graphy.)

BETWEEN THE SEXES

Your lips are like wet liver.

Deine Lippen sind so zart wie nasse Leber.

(Dyne lippn zind zo tsart vee nasse layber.)

Act like a human being!

Benimm Dich wie ein Mensch.

(Benimm deesh vee yn mensh.)

Act like a human being!

FRENCH	ITALIAN	SPANISH
Vous vous spécialisez dans la pornographie?	Vendete esclusivamente letteratura pornografica?	¿Sólo vende pornografia?
(Voo voo spaiseeahleezay dan lar pornografee?)	*(Vend-eh-teh esclusiv-ah-meh-nteh let-teh-rahtóo-rah pornográphy-cah?)*	*(Sóloh béndeh pornogra-pheeya?)*

| Vous avez les lèvres comme du foie meurtri! | Le tue labbra sono come fegato crudo. | Tus labios son como la hiel. |
| *(Voo zavay lay laivr kom di fwar mehrtree!)* | *(Leh too-eh lah-brah sono comeh féh-gah-to croo-do.)* | *(Toos lábbyos són cómoh lá yél.)* |

| Et si vous cessiez de vous conduire comme un ani-mal? | Si comporti da essere umano. | Pórtate como un ser hu-mano. |
| *(Eh see voo saisyay d'voo condweer kom an aneemal?)* | *(See com-port-ee dah eh-ssehreh oo-mahno.)* | *(Pórtahte cómoh oon sér oománoh.)* |

111

BETWEEN THE SEXES

Get lost.

Hau'ab.
(Hao aap.)

Is that gray hair or dandruff?

Sind das graue Haare oder Schuppen?
(Zind daass grou-e haare odr shooppn?)

When did they let you out of your cage?

Seit wann lässt man Dich frei rumlaufen?
(Zyt van laysst man deesh fry roomlaofen?)

Flea powder is cheap, you know.

Flohpuder ist billig.
(Flopoodr ist billig.)

Go jump in a lake.

Häng' Dich auf.
(Hayng deesh aof.)

THE MAILMAN

Do you enjoy reading all my mail?

Hat es Ihnen Spass gemacht, meine Post zu lesen?
(Haat es eenen shpaass gemacht, myne post tsoo laysn?)

How many deliveries a year do you make? Just this one?

Wie oft tragen Sie eigentlich Post aus, einmal in Jahr?
(Vee oft traagn zee ygentlish posst aos, ynmaal im yaar?)

FRENCH	ITALIAN	SPANISH
Allez vous faire voir! *(Allay voo fair vwar!)*	Va all'inferno. *(Vah ahll'in-ferno.)*	¡A ver si te pierdes de vista! *(A bér see té peeyérdes de beestah!)*
Vous grisonnez, ou ce sont simplement vos pellicules? *(Voo greezonay, oo sehr son samplerman vo pelleekil?)*	È forfora o sono capelli bianchi? *(Eh for-for-ah o sono cahpeh-llee bee-ahnkee?)*	¿Tienes los cabellos grises o llevas caspa? *(Teeyénes lóss cabéllyos greeses oh llyévas cáspah?)*
Il y a longtemps qu'on vous a sorti de votre cage? *(Eelyah lontan kon voo zar sorteed vawtr kash?)*	Quando l'hanno lasciato uscire dalla gabbia? *(Kwah-ndo l'ah-nno lah-shah-to oo-shee-reh dahllah gàh-bbea?)*	¿Cuándo te dejaron salir de la jáula? *(Kwándoh té déhháron saleer dé lá háoolah?)*
Le DDT n'est pas cher, vous savez! *(Lehr deh deh tay nay par shair, voo savay!)*	La polvere insetticida costa poco. *(Lah pol-veh-reh in-set-tee-chee-dah costah poco.)*	El polvo de pulgas es muy barato. *(El pólvoh dé poolgass éss mooy barátoh.)*
Allez vous faire pendre ailleurs! *(Allay voo fair pandr ayehr!)*	Vada a farsi friggere. *(Vahdah ah far-see free-dje-reh.)*	¡Tirate de cabeza al lago! *(Teerahte dé cabétha al lágoh!)*
J'espère que vous avez eu du plaisir à lire mes lettres? *(Shaispair ker voo zavay zi di plaizeer ar leer may lettr?)*	Si è divertito a leggere tutte le mie lettere? *(See eh dee-vert-ee-to ah leh-djeh-reh too-teh leh mee-eh let-teh-reh?)*	¿Le gusta leer mis cartas? *(Leh goostah lé-ér mees cártas?)*
Combien de fois passez-vous dans l'année—juste aujourd'hui? *(Kombyen der fwar passay-voo dan lannay—shist oshoordwee?)*	La posta la recapitate una volta l'anno? *(Lah post-a lah reh-cah-peetah-teh oona voltah l'ah-nno?)*	¿Cuántas cartas distribuye al año, una sola? *(Kwántas cártas distribooyeh ál ányo, oonah sólah?)*

113

THE PAINTER

How much water do you put in your paint?

Sie brauchen wohl viel Wasser zum Malen?

(Zee braochen vol feel vaasser tsoom maalen?)

Now wash your dirty fingerprints off the wall.

So jetzt wischen Sie Ihre dreckigen Fingerabdrücke von der Wand ab.

(Zo, yaytst veeshn zee eere draykigen fingerabdrueke fon dair vand aab.)

I asked you to paint it, not slosh it.

Malen sollten Sie das, nicht schmieren.

(Maalen zollten zee daass, nisht shmeeren.)

THE ELECTRICIAN

Do you cheat everyone who isn't an electrician?

Betrügen Sie jeden, der nichts von Elektrizität versteht?

(Betruegn zee yayden, dair nichts fon electritsitayt fershtayt?)

That's not a repair bill; it's a year's salary.

Das ist doch nicht die Rechnung, das muss Ihr Jahreseinkommen sein.

(Daass ist doch nisht dee rayshnoong, daass mooss eer yaaresynkommen syn.)

FRENCH	ITALIAN	SPANISH
Vous devez faire une de ces consommations d'eau dans votre peinture…!	Usate solo acqua per dipingere i muri?	¿Cuánta agua le ha puesto a esta pintura?
(Voo d'vay fair in der say consomahsyon do dan vawtr pantir…!)	*(Oo-zah-teh solo aqua per dee-peen-djereh ee moo-ree?)*	*(Kwántah ágwah lé ah pwéstoh á éstah peentoorah?)*
Enlevez-moi ces sales traces de doigts sur le mur.	E ora le dispiace togliere le sue sporche ditate dal muro?	A ver si quita las huellas que ha dejado en la pared.
(Anl'vay-mwar say sal trahs der dwah sir ler mir.)	*(Eh orah leh dees-pee-ah-cheh to-lee-eh-reh leh soo-eh spork-eh dee-tah-te dahl moo-ro?)*	*(Ah bér see keetah láss wéllyas ké ah dehhádoh én lá pahrét.)*
Vous appelez ça de la peinture, ce barbouillage?	Le ho chiesto di imbiancarlo, non di imbrattarlo.	Pedí que pintaran, no que salpicara la pared.
(Voo zapplay sar d'lar pantir, sehr barbooyash?)	*(Leh oh kee-ehsto dee imb-yank-ah-rlo, non dee imb-brah-tah-rlo.)*	*(Pehdi ké peentáran, noh ké salpeekáran lah pahrét.)*
Alors, comme ça, vous les roulez tous, ceux qui n'y connaissent rien à l'électricité?	Imbroglia proprio tutti quelli che di elettricità non se ne intendono?	¿Estafa usted a todos los que no entienden de electricidad?
(Alohr, komm sar, voo lay roolay toos, sehr kee nee connais ryen ar lelectreeceetay?)	*(Imb-broliah proh-pryo tootee kweh-llee keh dee elettri-chee-tah non seh neh intend-onoh?)*	*(Stáfah oostéh ah tóddos lóss ké nó enteeyénden dé electrithidát?)*
Vous appelez ça une facture, vous? C'est votre salaire annuel…!	Questo non è un conto riparazioni, è la sua paga annuale.	Esto no es la factura, es el sueldo de un año.
(Voo zapplay sar in faktir, voo? Say vawtr salair anniel…!)	*(Kwesto non eh oon coh-nto ree-pah-ratz-ee-onee, eh lah swa pah-gah ah-nnoo-ah-leh.)*	*(Estoh noh éss lah factoorah, éss él swéldoh dé oon ányo.)*

115

THE ELECTRICIAN

Wipe your dirty feet before you come in.

Wischen Sie sich Ihre Latschen ab, ehe Sie reinkommen.

(Veeshen zee zeesh dee laatshen aab, ayhe, zee rynkommen.)

THE ARCHITECT

I wanted a house, not a rabbit hutch.

Sie sollten ein Haus bauen und nicht einen Kaninchenstall.

(Zee zolten yn haos baon oon nisht ynen kaaneenshen-shtaall.)

I want the rain outside, not inside.

Aussen soll der Regen ablaufen, nicht innen.

(Aossen zol dair raygn ablaofen, nisht innen.)

I want the rain outside, not inside.

FRENCH	ITALIAN	SPANISH

Il y a un paillasson devant la porte!

(Eelyah an pa'yason d'van lar port!)

Prima di entrare abbia la decenza di pulirsi i piedi.

(Preema dee entr-ahreh ah-bya lah deh-chen-tza dee poo-leer-see ee pee-eh-dee.)

Límpiese las patas antes de entrar.

(Límpeeyese láss pátas ántess deh entrár.)

C'est une maison que je veux, pas un clapier!

(Say tin maison kersh vehr, pazan clapyay!)

Voglio una casa, non una conigliera.

(Vo-lio oona cah-sah, non oona co-nee-lee-eh-rah.)

Quería una casa, no una madriguera.

(Kereeya oonah cássah, noh oonah madreeguérah.)

Pourriez-vous faire en sorte que la pluie tombe à l'extérieur de cette pièce, plutôt qu'à l'intérieur?

(Pooryay-voo fair an sort ker lar plwee tomb ar lextairyehr der set peeais, plitaw kar lantairyehr?)

Dovrebbe piovere fuori, non dentro.

(Doh-vreh-beh pee-o-veh-reh foo-ohree, non dehn-tro.)

Quiero que llueva por fuera, no dentro de la habitación.

(Keeyéroh ké lluébah pór fooérah, noh déntroh dé lá abeetathión.)

THE ARCHITECT

Have you ever designed anything that works?

Haben Sie auch schon einmal etwas Brauchbares entworfen?

(Haabn zee aoch shon ynmaal etvaas braochbaares entvorfen?)

THE BUILDER

You've done a good job of hiding your mistakes.

Ich sehe, Sie haben Ihre fürchterliche Arbeit gut verputzt.

(Ish zaye, zee haaben eere fershterlishe aarbyt goot ferpootst.)

I asked for an estimate, not the first number that popped into your head.

Sagen Sie nicht, was Ihnen gerade in den Kopf kommt, sondern machen Sie einen Kostenanschlag.

(Zaagn zee nisht, vas eenen geraade in dayn kopf kommt, zondern maachn zee ynen kostenaanshlaag.)

How long do you guarantee it against collapse?

Wie lange garantieren Sie für den Bau bevor er einstürzt?

(Vee laange gaaraanteeren füer zee dayn bao befor er ynshtuertst?)

THE POLICEMAN

Excuse me, kind, brave, and gracious sir, but could you direct me to _____?

Entschuldigen Sie, bitte, verehrter, gütiger Herr, wie komme ich nach _____

(Endshooldign zee, bitte, ferairter, guetigr herr, vee komme ish naach _____

FRENCH	ITALIAN	SPANISH
Avez-vous jamais construit quelque chose qui tienne debout?	È mai riuscito a costruire qualcosa che funziona?	¿Ha diseñado alguna vez algo que sirva?
(*Avay-voo shahmay construee kelk'er shoz kee tyen derboo?*)	(*Eh my ree-oo-shee-to ah costr-oo-ee-reh kwahl-co-sah keh foon-tzee-onah?*)	(*Ah deesehnyádo algoonah béth álgoh ké seerbah?*)
Y a pas à dire, ça, c'est du beau camouflage! C'est dix fois mieux que le travail salopé qu'il y a dessous!	Bravo, è riuscito a nascondere tutte le sue magagne.	Veo que ya ha cubierto su horrible casucha.
(*Yah pazah deer, sar, say di bo camouflage! Say dee fwar myehr ker lehr travah'ee sahlopay keel yah dersoo!*)	(*Bravo, eh reè-oo-shee-to ah nah-scond-ehre too-teh leh soo-eh mah-gahn-yeh.*)	(*Béoh ké yá ah coobeeyér-toh soo orreebleh casoot-chah.*)
Je vous ai demandé un devis, pas une devinette!	Volevo un preventivo, non la prima cifra che le è passata per la testa.	Le pedi un presupuesto, no la primera cifra que se le ocurriese.
(*Sher voo zay d'manday an dervee, pazin derveenett!*)	(*Voh-leh-vo oon preh-vent-eevo, non lah preemah chee-frah keh leh eh pass-ahtah per lah teh-stah.*)	(*Leh peddee oon presupooé-stoh, noh lá preemérah thee-frah ké sé lé okoorryyéseh.*)
Ça mettra combien de temps à s'effondrer?	Quanto c'è di garanzia prima che crolli?	¿Lo garantiza usted antes de que se derrumbe?
(*Sar metrah kombyen der tan ar seffondray?*)	(*Kwah-nto cheh dee gah-rahn-tzeea preemah keh cro-lleee?*)	(*Loh gárénteetha oostéh ántes dé ké sé derrumbeh?*)
Auriez-vous l'amabilité de m'indiquer le chemin pour aller à—?	Mi scusi, gentiluomo, mi portrebbe indicare la strada per _____?	Perdone, amable, valiente y gracioso señor: ¿Quiere enseñarme por dónde se va a _____?
(*Auryay-voo lammabeelee-tay d'mandeekay l'sherman poor allay ar___?*)	(*Meé scoo-see, gent-eel-oo-ohmo, mee poh-tre-bbeh in-dee-cah-reh lah strada per _____?*)	(*Perdóneh, amabbleh, buh-leeyénte ee grathiósoh senyór: Keeyéreh ensenyarmeh pór dóndeh sé bá ah lá pórrah?*)

119

AT THE LAUNDRY

Those smelly rags aren't mine.

Diese übelriechenden Fetzen ge-
hören nicht mir.
*(Deeze uebl-reeshenden faytsen ge-
hoeren nisht meer.)*

**Your grubby staff must have been
wearing my shirts.**

Ihr dreckiges Personal hat meine
Hemden getragen.
*(Eer drayckiges pairsonaal haat
myne haymden getraagen.)*

Don't you use soap?

Benutzen Sie keine Seife?
(Benootsen zee kyne zyfe?)

These used to be my buttons.

Und diese kleinen Dinger waren
meine Knöpfe.
*(Oond deeze klynen Deenger vaaren
myne cnoep-fe.)*

Can't you count?

Können Sie nicht zählen?
(Koennen zee nisht tsaylen?)

ALL-PURPOSE INSULTS

Long-haired creep.

Oller Leisetreter.
(Oller lysetraiter.)

Hairy ape.

Behaarter Affe.
(Behaarter aaffe.)

Useless imbecile.

Blöder Trottel
(Bloeder trottl.)

FRENCH	ITALIAN	SPANISH
Elles ne sont pas à moi, ces vieilles nippes crasseuses! *(Ell ner son paza mwar, say vyey neep krasserz!)*	Questa roba puzzolente non è mia. *(Kwesta roba poo-tzo-lehn-teh non eh mee-ah.)*	Estos trapos sucios no son míos. *(Éstos tráposs sootheeyos noh són meeyos.)*
Vos sales employés se sont servis de mes chemises! *(Vo sal zamplwayay s'son sairvee d'may shermeez!)*	Le mie camicie le ha indossate un vostro sudicio dipendente? *(Leh mee-eh cah-mee-cheh leh ah in-doss-ah-teh oon vo-stro sóo-dée-choh dee-pendeh-nteh?)*	Sus empleados deben haberse puesto mis camisas. *(Soos empleádos dében abérseh pwésto mees cameesas.)*
Vous ne vous servez jamais de savon? *(Voon voo sairvay sharmay der savon?)*	Il sapone non lo usate? *(Eel sah-poneh non lo oo-zah-teh?)*	¿No emplea jabón para lavar? *(Noh empléah habbón párah lábár?)*
C'était mes boutons, ces petits morceaux d'écaille! *(Saitay may booton, say p'tee morso daikah'ee.)*	Questi frammenti erano i miei bottoni. *(Kweh-stee frah-ment-ee eh rah-no ee mee-eh-ee boh-tto-nee.)*	Estos residuos eran mis botones. *(Estos rreseeduous éran mees botóness.)*
Vous ne savez pas compter? *(Voon savay par kontay?)*	Non sa contare? *(Non sah cont-ah-re?)*	¡No sabe contar! *(Noh sábeh contár!)*
Crétin à crinière. *(Craitan ar creenyair.)*	Ebete capelluto. *(Eh-beh-teh capehl-loo-toh.)*	Animal de bellotas. *(Annimál deh behlyótass.)*
Troglodyte. *(Troglodeet.)*	Stupido scimmione. *(Stoopeedoh sheemee-ohneh.)*	Espantapájaros. *(Spantahpáhharos.)*
Imbécile. *(Ambaiseel.)*	Imbecille buon a nulla. *(Eembeh-cheeleh boo-ohn ah noolla.)*	Cretino. *(Creteenoh.)*

ALL-PURPOSE INSULTS

Incompetent lout.	Ungeschickter Trampel. *(Oongeshickter traampl.)*
Drooling, senile, old fool.	Blöder Sabberer. *(Bloeder zaabberer.)*
Narrow-minded idiot.	Bornierter Lackel. *(Borneerter lakl.)*
Moron.	Nackter Wilder. *(Naackter veelder.)*
Ass.	Narr. *(Naarr.)*
Donkey.	Esel. *(Ayzel.)*
Touched in the head.	Schwach im Kopf. *(Shvaach im kopf.)*
Scatterbrain.	Dölmer. *(Doelmer.)*
Useless.	Unbrauchbar. *(Oonbraochbaar.)*
Bonkers.	Blöde. *(bloede.)*
Brainless.	Verblödet. *(Ferbloedet.)*
Senseless.	Sinnlos. *(Zinnlos.)*
Pig-headed.	Dickkopfig. *(Dickoepfig.)*
Blundering idiot.	Stupider Holzkopf. *(Shtoopeeder holtskopf.)*
Feeble-minded fool.	Schwachsinniger Blödkopf. *(Shvaachzinniger Bloedkopf.)*

FRENCH	ITALIAN	SPANISH
Vaurien. *(Voryen.)*	Zoticone inetto. *(Zohteeconeh in-eht-toh.)*	Piojo indecente. *(Peeyóhho indethénteh.)*
Vieux baveux. *(Vyer bavehr.)*	Stupido vecchio rincitrullito. *(Stoopeedoh veh-keeoh reen-chee-trool-leeto.)*	Viejo baboso. *(Beeyéhho babbósoh.)*
Borné. *(Bornay.)*	Idiota meschino. *(Idiot-ah meh-skee-noh.)*	Despreciable idiota *(Desprethiábleh eediótah.)*
Crétin. *(Craitan.)*	Deficiente. *(Deh-fee-chenteh.)*	Carcamal. *(Carcamáhll.)*
Ane bâté. *(Ann battay.)*	Somaro. *(Soh-mah-roh.)*	Asno. *(Assnoh.)*
Bourricot. *(Booreeko.)*	Asino. *(Ah-zeenoh.)*	Burro. *(Boorroh.)*
Dingue. *(Dang.)*	Pazzoide. *(Pah-tzo-ee-deh.)*	Majareta. *(Mahharétah.)*
Ecervelé. *(Aiservelay.)*	Scervellato. *(Sher-vehl-latoh.)*	Memo. *(Méhmoh.)*
Bon à rien. *(Bon aryen.)*	Incapace. *(In-cah-pah-cheh.)*	Bobo. *(Bóbboh.)*
Cinglé. *(Sanglay.)*	Alienato. *(Ah-lee-eh-nato.)*	Botarate. *(Bawtaráteh.)*
Tête d'épingle. *(Tait daipangl.)*	Testa vuota. *(Teh-stah voo-oh-ta.)*	Mentecato. *(Mentehkátoh.)*
Insensé. *(Ansansay.)*	Insensato. *(In-sehn-sah-to.)*	Zopenco. *(Thopénkoh.)*
Tête de mule. *(Tait der mil.)*	Testardo. *(Teh-star-doh.)*	Fantoche. *(Phantótcheh.)*
Balourd. *(Bahloor.)*	Cretino confusionario. *(Creh-tee-noh cohn-foo-zeeo-nareeo.)*	Papanatas. *(Pápahnátas.)*
Vieille cloche. *(Vyey klosh.)*	Scemo innato. *(Sheh-moh in-nato.)*	Ignorante. *(Iggnohránteh.)*

ALL-PURPOSE INSULTS

Thick-skinned pachyderm.

Dickfelliges Nilpferd.
(Dickfaylliges neelpfaird.)

Miss Proper.

Gezierter Käfer.
(Getseerter kayfer.)

Mentally retarded.

Schwachsinnig.
(Shvachzinnig.)

Smelly fool.

Widerlicher Kerl.
(Veederlisher kairl.)

Perfumed pansy.

Parfümierter Schwuler.
(Paarfuemeerter shvooler.)

Chinless wonder.

Doofes Gestell.
(Doves geshtell.)

Mind of a child.

Kindliches Gemüt.
(kindlishes gemuet.)

Lying loafer.

Verlogener Rumtreiber.
(Ferlogener roomtryber.)

Thieving hound.

Elender Betrüger.
(Aylender betrueger.)

Sticky-fingered

Klebrig. *(klaybrig.)*

FRENCH	ITALIAN	SPANISH
Grosse brute. *(Gross britt.)*	Pachiderma insensibile. *(Pah-kee-derma in-sehn-see-bee-leh.)*	Caradura *(Karahdoorah.)*
Vieille tata *(to a man)* or Chipie *(to a woman).* *(Vyey tata—Sheepee.)*	Signorinella in punta di forchetta. *(See-neeo-ree-nehlla in poonta dee for-kehtta.)*	Niña piripi. *(Neenya peer-eepee.)*
Arriéré. *(Aryeray.)*	Menomato mentale. *(Meh-noh-mah-to mental-eh.)*	Retrasado mental. *(Retra-sádoh mentáhl.)*
Ours puant. *(Oors pi'an.)*	Stupido puzzolente. *(Stoo-peedo pootzoh-lehnteh.)*	Pazguato. *(Pathgwátoh.)*
Tata de luxe. *(Tata der luxe.)*	Damerino profumato. *(Dah-meh-reeno proh-foomahto.)*	Marica. *(Marykah.)*
Dégénéré. *(Deshenairay.)*	Aristocraticone. *(Aristo-crateeconeh.)*	Mariquita. *(Marykeetah.)*
Infantile. *(Anfanteel.)*	Cervello di gallina. *(Chehrvehl-loh dee gahl-leena.)*	Pusilánime. *(Poosillani-meh.)*
Fieffé menteur. *(Fyeffay 'mantehr.)*	Vitellone bugiardo. *(Vee-tehl-loneh boojardoh.)*	Zoquete. *(Thokéhteh.)*
Chien de voleur. *(Shyen der volehr.)*	Ladro malandrino. *(Lah-dro mah-lahn-dreeno.)*	Fullero. *(Foolyéroh.)*
Poisseux. *(Pwasehr.)*	Mano lesta. *(Mah-noh leh-sta.)*	Bandido. *(Bandídoh.)*

ALL-PURPOSE INSULTS

Insensitive idiot.

Gefühlloser idiot.
(*Gefuehlloser eediot.*)

Nonsense!

Unsinn. (*Oonzinn.*)

Babbling fool.

Alter Sabberer.
(*Aalter zaberer.*)

Old windbag.

Bösartige alte Klatsche.
(*Boesaartige aalte Klaatshe.*)

Immoral.

Unmoralisch. (*Oonmohraalish.*)

Obscene pig.

Zotig. (*Tsotig.*)

Bald-headed coot.

Geruptftes Huhn.
(*Geroopftes Hoon.*)

Gorilla.

Haariger Affe. (*Haareeger Aaffe.*)

Old hag.

Saure Ziege. (*Zaore tseege.*)

Scarecrow.

Vogelscheuche. (*Foglshoiche.*)

FRENCH	ITALIAN	SPANISH
Brute. *(Britt.)*	Idiota senza cuore. *(Idiotah sehntza kworeh.)*	Bobalicón. *(Bobbahlikón.)*
Foutaise. *(Footaiz.)*	Sciocchezze. *(Shock-kehtzeh.)*	Babieca. *(Babbyékah.)*
Clabaudeur. *(Clabodehr.)*	Chiacchierone incoerente. *(Kiak-keh-roneh in-coehrehnteh.)*	Imbécil. *(Imbéthill.)*
Pipelette venimeuse. *(Peeplet verneemerz.)*	Pettegola maligna. *(Pehtteh-gola mah-lee-neeah.)*	Chismoso. *(Cheesmósoh.)*
Immoral. *(Eemorahl.)*	Immorale. *(Immoral-eh.)*	Indecente. *(Indehthenteh.)*
Obscène. *(Obsain.)*	Volgarone osceno. *(Volgahroneh oh-sheh-no.)*	Cochino. *(Cotcheenoh.)*
Tête d'œuf. *(Tait derf.)*	Testa pelata. *(Teh-sta pehlah-ta.)*	Cateto. *(Katétoh.)*
Gorille. *(Goreey.)*	Scimmione irsuto. *(Sheemmeeo-neh eersootoh.)*	Mono peludo. *(Mónoh pehloodoh.)*
Vieille mégère. *(Vyey meshair.)*	Zitella inacidita. *(Tzeetehl-la in-ah-chee-deeta.)*	Cara de vinagre. *(Kárah deh beennágrre.)*
Epouvantail. *(Epoovanta'ee.)*	Spaventapasseri. *(Spavehntah-passehree.)*	Bruja. *(Broohha.)*